QUILTAGAMI

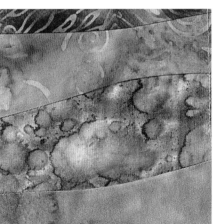

QUILTAGAMI
THE ART OF FABRIC FOLDING

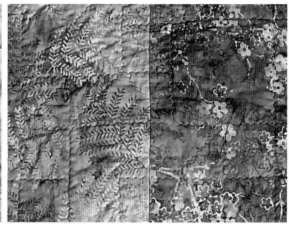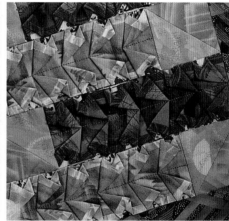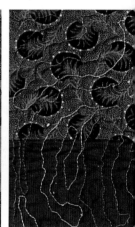

MARY JO HINEY

STERLING PUBLISHING CO., INC. NEW YORK
A STERLING/CHAPELLE BOOK

CHAPELLE, LTD.

Owner: Jo Packham

Editor: Karmen Quinney

Staff: Areta Bingham, Kass Burchett, Ray Cornia, Marilyn Goff, Karla Haberstich, Holly Hollingsworth, Susan Jorgensen, Barbara Milburn, Caroll Shreeve, Cindy Stoeckl, Kim Taylor, Sara Toliver, Desirée Wybrow

Photo Stylist: Jill Dahlberg

Photography: Kevin Dilley for Hazen Photography

Library of Congress Cataloging-in-Publication Data Available

10 9 8 7 6 5 4 3

A Sterling/Chapelle Book

First paperback edition published in 2003 by
Sterling Publishing Co., Inc.
387 Park Avenue South, New York, NY 10016
© 2002 by Mary Jo Hiney
Distributed in Canada by Sterling Publishing
C/o Canadian Manda Group, 165 Dufferin Street,
Toronto, Ontario, Canada M6K 3H6
Distributed in Great Britain by Chrysalis Books Group PLC,
The Chrysalis Building, Bramley Road, London W10 6SP, England.
Distributed in Australia by Capricorn Link (Australia) Pty. Ltd.
P.O. Box 704, Windsor, NSW 2756, Australia

Printed in China
All Rights Reserved

Sterling ISBN 0-8069-8279-9 Hardcover
              1-4027-0859-9 Paperback

For information about custom editions, special sales, premium and corporate purchases, please contact Sterling Special Sales Department at 800-805-5489 or specialsales@sterlingpub.com

If you have any questions or comments, please contact:

Chapelle, Ltd., Inc.
P.O. Box 9252
Ogden, UT 84409
Phone: (801) 621-2777
FAX: (801) 621-2788
e-mail: chapelle@chapelleltd.com
web site: www.chapelleltd.com

Resources for Origami Folds:
The Great Origami Book, by Zülal Aytüre Scheele, 1987, Sterling Publishing, New York

The Joy of Origami, by Toshie Takahama, 1985, Shufunotomo Co., Ltd. Tokyo

Omiyage, by Kumiko Sudo, 2001, Contemporary Books, Chicago

TABLE OF CONTENTS

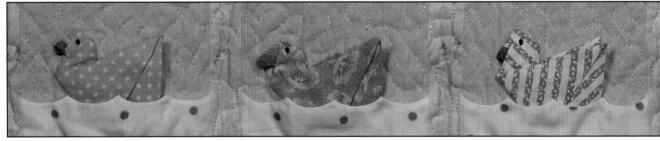

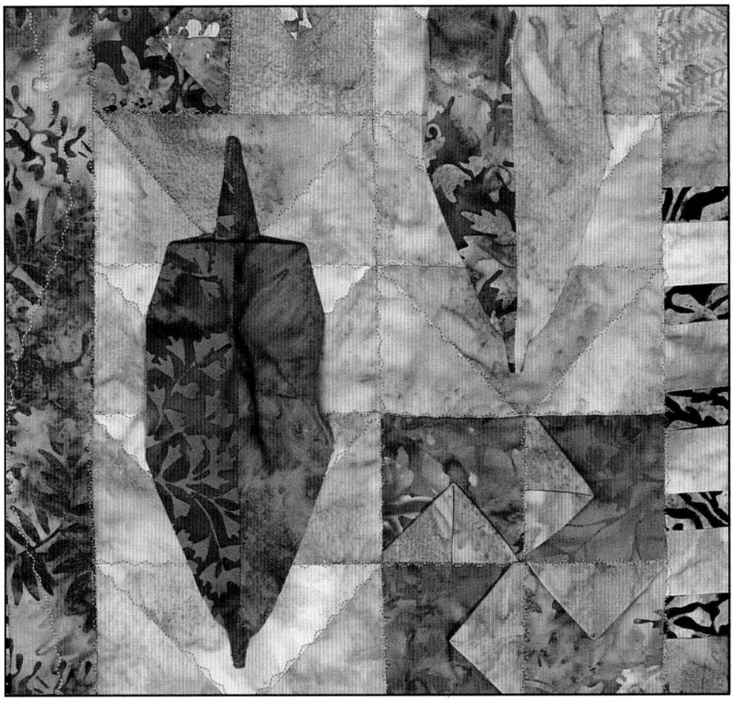

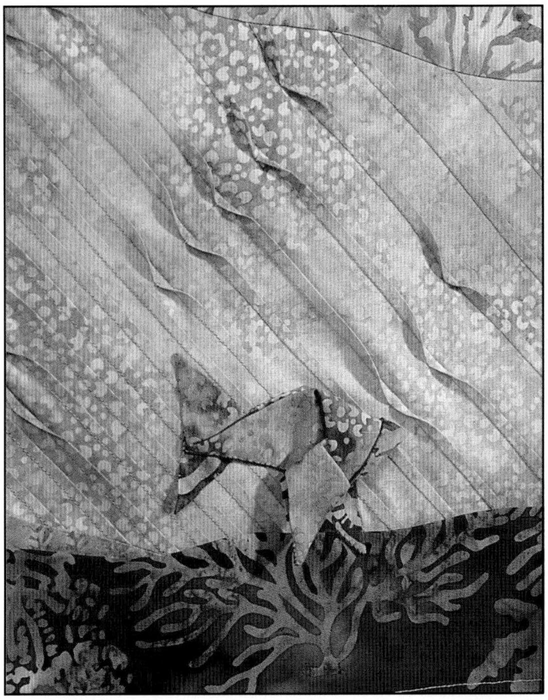

GENERAL INSTRUCTIONS

Fabric Variations

QUILTAGAMI:

Quiltagami is the art of folding and stitching fabric—origami style. The folded and stitched fabric is then assembled into blocks for quilting.

Quilters and origami enthusiasts have an opportunity with Mary Jo Hiney's *Quiltagami* to merge the two art forms into an altogether new textile art.

The traditions of beautiful fabric selections in harmonizing patterns and colors, accurate stitching, and the meticulous assembly and finishing techniques of quilting are paired with the precise valley-and-mountain folding techniques of Japanese origami figures.

Forms of animals, leaves, flowers, and people, created for centuries in Japan from two-colored squares of paper have been reinterpreted in fabric relief by Mary Jo. She has artfully embellished quilt blocks with her quiltagami designs to create exquisitely stitched, practical, and fanciful items for the home and to wear.

The tactile delights of sculptural quiltagami figures appear to come to life on pillows, blankets, and decorative items. There is an irresistible desire on the viewer's part to touch the flowers, feel the separate petals and leaves, and perhaps to take the figure of a crawling child out of a quilt pocket and hold it on their palm for closer inspection.

Bead and ribbon embellishments add exquisite detail to folded and stitched quiltagami figures. With Mary Jo's instructions and examples, the quilter's scrap box and imagination are resources for an entirely new fabric art form.

Unfinished quilt blocks in the studio setting suggest optional ideas for how to use her basic fold-and-stitch techniques in imaginative ways on items the reader creates.

NEEDED SUPPLIES FOR QUILTAGAMI:

Following are supplies that every quilter should have on hand before beginning, along with required fabrics and notions for each project:

- Copier paper
- Cutting mat
- Fabric marker
- Fabric scissors
- Fabric starch
- Freezer paper
- Glue stick
- Iron/ironing board
- Mylar® or pattern marker
- Pencil, #2
- Quilter's ruler
- Quilting needles
- Quilting pins
- Rotary cutter
- Sewing machine
- Sewing needles
- Spray bottle/water
- Tape measure
- Tear-away paper
- Tracing paper

BASIC ORIGAMI:

To learn origami, all you really need is a sheet of paper or scrap of fabric. Practice all folding techniques before beginning. Pressing and starching all fabric will make the folding process easier and produce a better final result. The following list of tools, products, and materials will help you make the most of your origami quilting experience.

Creasing Tools:

• **Fingers** are excellent for making sharp creases. Pinch fabric crease lightly between thumbnail and forefinger and move along the edge of a fold to make a sharp, clean crease. This method also comes in handy with relaxing an open crease. You can also create sharp creases by laying the folded fabric on a hard flat surface and running your middle finger and forefinger along the edges of the fold.

• **Wooden skewers** come in handy for gently pushing folded corners and points out. These tools become especially useful when folding tiny pieces of origami.

• **Fusible webbing** is great for stiffening material and also for ironing materials together. Fusible webbing can be used with a wide assortment of fabrics. Make certain that the fabrics are iron-safe before applying fusible webbing.

• **Fabric starches** come in sprays and are used to make fabrics easier to handle. Spray starch and ironing is a fast and easy method to fold fabrics into crisp origami shapes. Spray fabric stiffener and blow-drying are used to preserve and harden fabric and can also

be used in wet-folding techniques to shape, harden, and preserve many types of fabric.

Techniques to Know:

• **Basic folds** are common folding techniques to make various basicly folded forms that can then be sculpted into other forms. Basic folds save time and space in having to repeat a common set of preliminary folds. Some of the popular forms include square or crane base, butterfly or letter base, kabuto or turtle base, pinwheel base, fish base, cootie base, and other simple forms. Bases may have other names, depending upon the origami instructor. Some instructors simply number their basic folds.

• **Creases, precreases, and sharp creases** make a big difference in the final appearance of an origami model. Precreases are soft creases that make folding fabric along a crease line easier to see and do, as a set of folding techniques progresses.

• **Pleats** require convex and concave folds to shape delicate curves into origami.

Basic Origami Folds:

• Fold and Unfold:

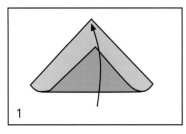

1 Turn square of fabric around to look like a diamond. Valley-fold it in half diagonally from bottom to top, forming a triangle. Press flat.

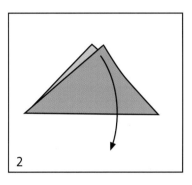

2 Unfold triangle completely.

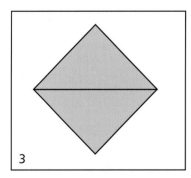

3 This is the completed fold and unfold. A solid line represents an existing fold line, i.e. one that is the result of a previous step.

• Inside-reverse Fold:

This technique gets its name because the fabric being folded moves inside and a ridge is reversed from a mountain to a valley fold.

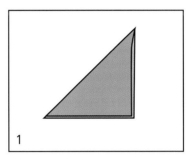

1 Fold fabric square in half to make a triangle. Insert thumb between right-hand layers of fabric and at the same time place your forefinger on triangle ridge.

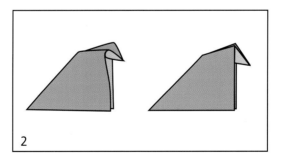

2 Draw back your forefinger and at the same time push down on ridge, reversing it into a valley fold.

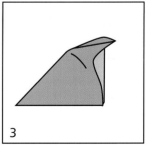

3 Press fabric flat, completing inside-reverse fold.

• Mountain Fold:

This technique gets its name because the fabric is being folded to make a convex crease that resembles a mountain.

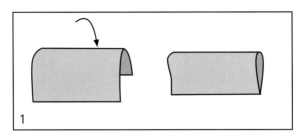 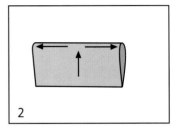

1 Hold bottom edge of fabric square. Bend top edge backward and take it down to meet bottom edge.

2 Keeping edges to- gether, run your thumb up the center of paper to top edge. Run your thumb and fingers along top edge, completing fold.

• Open and Squash:

This technique is named such because layers of fabric, or a pocket, have been opened out and squashed down.

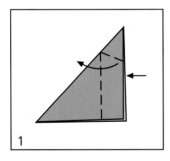 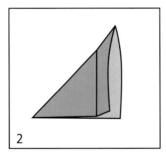 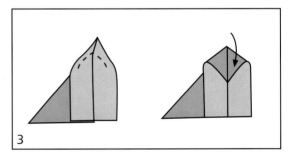

1 Valley-fold fabric square in half diagonally from top left to bottom right, forming a triangle.

2 Valley-fold from right-hand side over toward left (exact position is not impor- tant). Press top layer flat and open it up along fold line that has just been made. Insert your fingers between layers of fabric.

3 With your hand, squash layers down neatly into this shape. Press fabric flat, completing open-and-squash technique.

• Valley Fold:

This technique gets its name because the fabric is being folded to make a concave crease that resembles a valley.

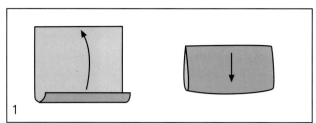 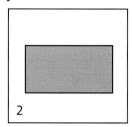

1 Hold top edge of fabric square. Lift bottom edge up to meet top edge. Keeping edges together, run your forefinger down the center of the fabric to bottom edge.

2 Run your fingers along bottom edge of both sides, completing fold.

BASIC QUILTING:

Backing:

Use cotton fabric for quilt backing. If hand-sewing quilt, avoid bed sheets for backing. They are difficult to quilt through. When making a bed-sized quilt, the fabric may need to be pieced to fit the quilt top.

Fabrics:

The fabrics used in the projects are all cotton. These wash well and hold a crease while folding the pieces. All fabrics should be tested for colorfastness or prewashed before assembling the quilts.

Cutting Fabrics:

When cutting squares for folding, accuracy and cutting on the grain are important.

Tearing of fabric is not recommended because of the ragged edges it creates.

Batting:

Batting is traditionally used as the middle layer of a quilt, and sometimes in clothing and dollmaking. There are numerous types of batting available. Bonded cotton batting gives a flat, natural appearance and will require a great deal of quilting to secure layers, with quilting lines less than 1" apart. Felt may be substituted and renders the same appearance as bonded cotton. Polyester batting gives a puffy appearance and is a good choice for machine-quilting. *Note: All of these quilts were machine-quilted.* Thick batting is recommended for tied quilts.

Tip:

Remove batting from the package a day before using. Open it out to full size. This will help the batting lie flat.

Foundation Piecing:

Foundation fabrics must be stable enough to stitch fabric pieces onto and sheer enough to see through. Examples of good foundation fabrics are muslin, paper, tearaway backing, and lightweight interfacing. If a permanent foundation fabric is used, this will add an extra piece of fabric to quilt through.

Foundation piecing often requires preseaming. Preseaming means that two pieces of fabric may need to be stitched together before being stitched to the foundation. The fabrics must be cut to the shape of the area and sewn together. They are then treated as one unit, with the seam resting on the appropriate seam line.

For foundation piecing, pieces need not be cut perfectly. Use strips, rectangles, squares, or any odd-shaped scrap material. Make certain fabric is at least ⅜" larger on all sides than the area it is to cover. As triangle shapes are more difficult to piece, use generously sized fabric pieces and position pieces carefully on the foundation. Some fabric is wasted in foundation piecing, but the time saved is well worth the results.

Mirror Image:

Foundation quilting will create a mirror image of the pattern. If an exact replica of the pattern is desired, reverse the pattern on the foundation, following the method for mirrored-image units. This book has been designed so each set of patterns and instructions will result in an exact image of the photograph shown.

Many of the quilt blocks in *Quiltagami* have left and right mirrored units. Only one pattern is given. Trace two unit patterns, but make one unit pattern on the wrong side. This is just one advantage to using a see-through foundation. If a see-through foundation is not used, make a copy of the pattern. Flip the paper over and hold it up to a light source, then trace onto foundation.

Foundation Piecing Instructions:

1 Transfer pattern onto foundation, as shown in photo below. Using a #2 pencil, write all numbers on foundation. Mark for a mirror image, if applicable.

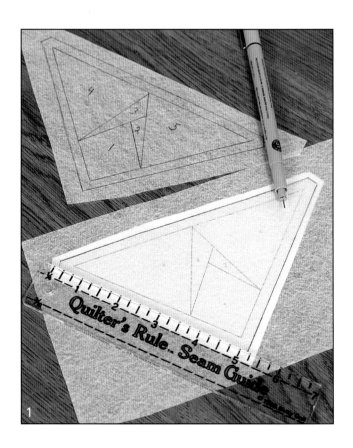

2 Cut fabric pieces for block. Make a chart as an aid to note fabrics, number placements, cut sizes and quantities needed for each fabric.

3 Turn over foundation with unmarked side up. Place fabric piece 1, right side up, on shape 1. If foundation is not sheer, hold foundation up to a light source to make certain that fabric overlaps at least ¼" on all sides of shape 1. Pin, glue, or hold in place.

4 Make certain that fabric piece 2 overlaps at least ¼" on all sides of shape 2. Place fabric piece 2 on fabric piece 1, right sides together.

5 Turn over foundation, with marked side up. Sew along line between shapes 1 and 2, using a very small stitch as shown in photo at right. *Note: This is helpful if paper has been used as the foundation.* Begin and end two or three stitches beyond line.

6 Trim excess fabric ⅛" – ¼" past seam line as shown in photo at right. Take care not to cut foundation.

7 Turn over foundation, with unmarked side up. Open fabric piece 2 and finger-press seam. Pin or glue in place, if necessary.

8 Make certain that fabric piece 3 overlaps at least ¼" on all sides of shape 3 as shown in photo at right. Place fabric piece 3 on fabric piece 1, with right sides together. Secure in place. Repeat Steps 5–6.

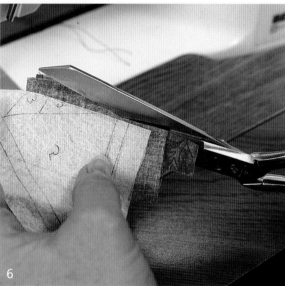

EVENING SKY PILLOW

ONE SEES THE SKY
THROUGH A HOLLOW
REED.

FABRICS:

Note: All fabrics are 42"–45" wide.

Blue (nine different variations)

- Four variations of blue (¼ yd each) for Shimmer Star Block, Faceted Star Block
- Blue (½ yd) for center portion of band, band backing
- Blue (¾ yd) for Shimmer Star Block, inside band backing
- Three variations of blue (⅛ yd each) for Shimmer Star Block

Ecru (one variation)

- Ecru (¼ yd) for Shimmer Star Block, side edge pillow band

Gold (four different variations)

- Two variations of gold (¼ yd each) for Shimmer Star Block
- Gold (1¼ yd) for Shimmer Star Block, pillow case
- Gold (⅛ yd) for Shimmer Star Block

Rust (two different variations)

- Two variations of rust (¼ yd each) for Shimmer Star Block

NOTIONS:

Beads: 6mm, blue (6)

Cord: blue (2 yds); gold (2 yds)

Cover buttons: ½" dia. (2)

Nonwoven interfacing or broadcloth (1 yd) for foundation

Pillow form: 20"

SHIMMER STAR BLOCK (A):

3 Using gold fabrics, make six of **Star in Square**, following Steps 1–7 on opposite page. Appliqué one in center of each **Shimmer Star Block**. Stitch 6mm bead in center of each **Star in Square**.

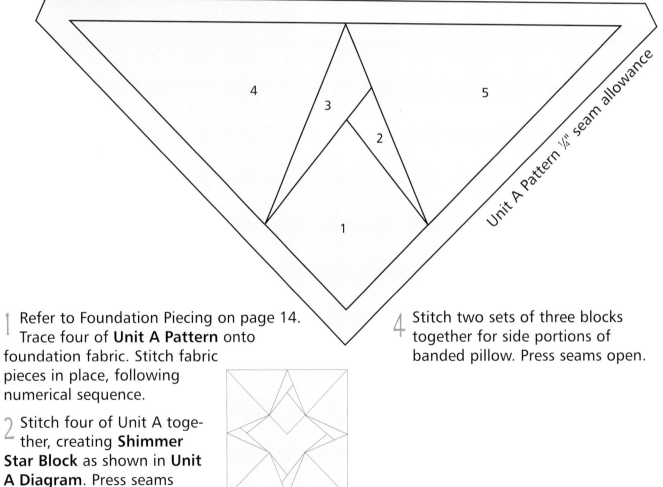

4

3

2

5

1

Unit A Pattern ¼" seam allowance

1 Refer to Foundation Piecing on page 14. Trace four of **Unit A Pattern** onto foundation fabric. Stitch fabric pieces in place, following numerical sequence.

2 Stitch four of Unit A together, creating **Shimmer Star Block** as shown in **Unit A Diagram**. Press seams open. Repeat five times for six blocks.

Unit A Diagram

4 Stitch two sets of three blocks together for side portions of banded pillow. Press seams open.

STAR IN SQUARE:

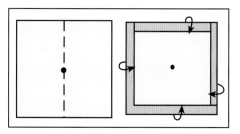

1 Cut one 4½" square from gold fabric. Fold to mark center. Press all edges under ¼".

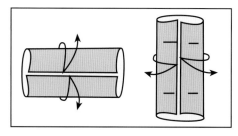

2 Press to center, unfold. Fold other sides to center, press middle, unfold.

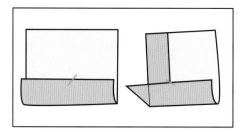

3 Fold up bottom edge, stitch center to marked center. Rotate. Fold up bottom edge, stitch center to marked center. Rotate.

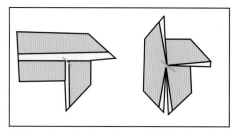

4 Fold up bottom edge, stitch center to marked center. Fold up remaining edge, stitch center to marked center. Press edges flat.

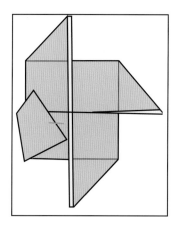

5 Fold up corner by pushing down point. Tack.

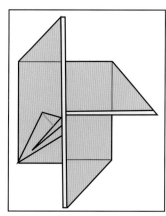

6 Fold opposite corner by pushing down point. Tack.

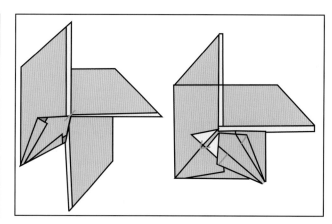

7 Stitch into tip of upper point, bring down to center. Tack and rotate. Repeat Steps 5–6, then stitch into tip of upper point, bring down to center. Tack and rotate. Repeat Steps 5–7 two times for Star in Square. Make two of Star in Square.

FACETED STAR BLOCK (B):

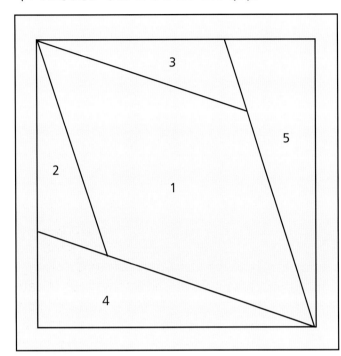

Unit B Pattern ¼" seam allowance

4 Trace four of **Faceted Star Corner Pattern (B2)** on page 21 onto foundation fabric. Stitch fabric pieces in place, following numerical sequence. *Note: Pieces 4 and 4a are preseamed before being sewn in place.*

5 Stitch **Faceted Star Blocks**, **Halves**, and **Corners** together as shown in **Pillow Diagram**. Press seams open.

6 Using blue fabrics, make two Dusk Stars, following Steps 1–9 on page 22. Appliqué one **Dusk Star** diagonally in center of each full-sized **Faceted Star Block**. Stitch covered button in center of each **Dusk Star**.

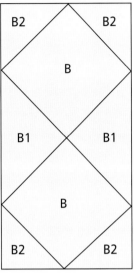

Pillow Diagram

Continued on page 23.

1 Refer to Foundation Piecing on page 14. Trace four of **Unit B Pattern** onto foundation fabric. Stitch fabric pieces in place, following numerical sequence.

2 Stitch four of Unit B together, creating **Faceted Star Block** as shown in **Unit B Diagram**. Press seams open. Repeat Steps 1–2 for two blocks.

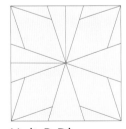

Unit B Diagram

3 Trace two of **Faceted Star Half Pattern (B1)** on page 21 onto foundation fabric. Stitch fabric pieces in place, following numerical sequence. *Note: Pieces 6, 6a, 7, and 7a are preseamed before being sewn in place.*

Dusk Star in Faceted Star Block

Faceted Star Half Pattern (B1) ¼" seam allowance

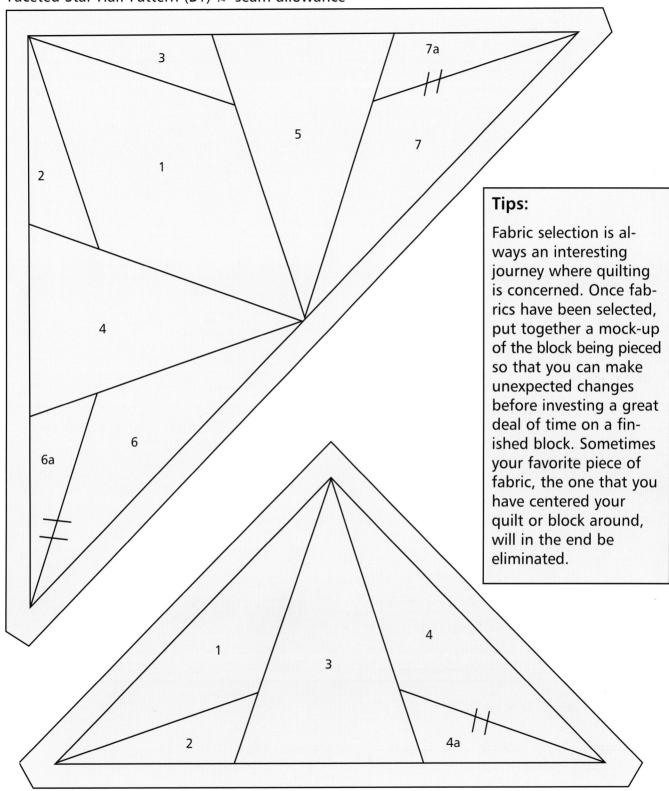

Tips:

Fabric selection is always an interesting journey where quilting is concerned. Once fabrics have been selected, put together a mock-up of the block being pieced so that you can make unexpected changes before investing a great deal of time on a finished block. Sometimes your favorite piece of fabric, the one that you have centered your quilt or block around, will in the end be eliminated.

Faceted Star Corner Pattern (B2) ¼" seam allowance

DUSK STAR:

Note: Dark and light shades do not denote right and wrong sides of fabric, but variations of color. Place fabric wrong side up to start folds.

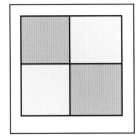

1 Cut four 3½" squares from two blue fabrics. Piece together squares, alternating shades. Press seams open. Trim to exactly 6" square. Press all edges under ¼". Repeat Steps 2–4 from **Star in Square** on page 19.

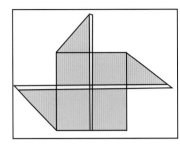

2 Flatten corner and press. Rotate.

3 Flatten corner and press. Rotate.

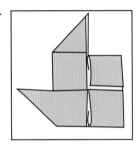

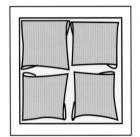

4 Repeat Step 3 two times.

5 Open out one corner and flatten. Invisibly stitch at center for ½".

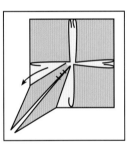

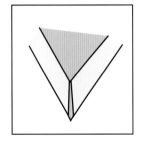

6 Refold bulk at outside tip.

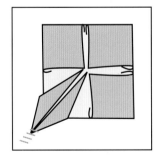

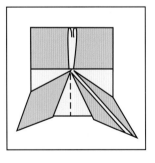

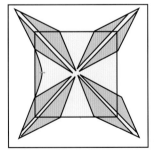

7 Fold tip in half, invisibly stitch tip together, then flatten tip.

8 Repeat Steps 5–7 for each tip.

9 Fold square side over ¼", tack at center. Make two of Dusk Star.

Continued from page 20.

7 Cut two 1" x 9" strips from blue fabric. Stitch to top and bottom of **Faceted Star Block** group. Press seams toward strip.

8 Stitch **Shimmer Star Block** to each side of **Faceted Star Block** group as shown in **Evening Star Pillow Diagram**. Press seams open.

Strip

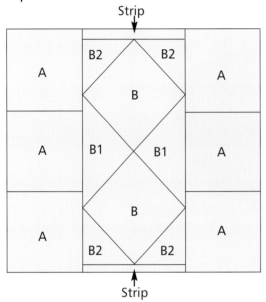

Strip

Evening Star Pillow Diagram

FINISHING BAND:

1 Cut two 11" x 20½" pieces from blue fabric for front. Stitch pieces to top and bottom of pieced band front. Press seams toward pieces.

2 Cut two 2" x 41" strips from blue fabric for backing. Stitch strips to band sides. Press seams toward strips.

3 Cut one 19¾" x 41" piece from ecru fabric. Place band front over backing, right sides together, matching long edges. Stitch long edges, taking a ¼" seam allowance. Repeat with opposite long edge. Press seams toward strips. Turn right side out. Position blue fabric so it is centered over band front. Press.

PILLOW CASE:

1 Cut one 36" x 41" piece from gold fabric. Match center of one end of band to center of 36" edge of gold fabric, positioning lining side of band against right side of gold fabric. Pin band to gold fabric. Repeat with opposite end of band and opposite edge of gold fabric.

2 Fold band/gold fabric in half, right sides together, matching pinned edges. Stitch, taking a ½" seam allowance, beginning and ending 2¼" from each end. Press seam open. Turn right side out.

3 Press one side edge under 1¼". Turn edge under again 1¼" and stitch close to pressed-under edge, forming pillow drawstring casing. Repeat with opposite side.

4 Insert cord into drawstring opening. Tie one end closed. Insert pillow form into pillow casing. Insert cord into opposite drawstring opening. Tie closed.

Note: Evening Sky Pillow contains six of Shimmer Star Block (A), two of Unit B, two of Faceted Star Half (B1), and four of Faceted Star Corner (B2).

23

This quilt block was created using Dusk Star instructions on page 22. Dusk Stars have been applied to triangles that have been sewn together to form four 4½" squares. These squares have been joined together to form one larger square. This quilt block could then be sewn together with others to form a larger quilt or with batting, backing, and binding used as a table trivet or a pot holder. It also could be applied to the front of a bag or an article of clothing.

This quilt block was created using the Star in Square instructions on page 19. In this piece the Star in Square fold has been used entirely to form a block. Nine of the Star in Square folds were made and stitched together to form a nine-patch. If made with a slightly heavier fabric, this could be used as a trivet on the table or backed with another fabric and batting. An entire quilt could be made of these nine-patch pieces. The initial pieces would not be as small and the result could be quite striking.

CALM OF LOTUS QUILT

FABRICS:

Note: All fabrics are 42"–45" wide.

Aqua (one variation)

- Aqua (⅛ yd) for Skinny Rose Block

Blue/Ecru (one variation)

- Blue/Ecru (¼ yd) for Border

Brown (three different variations)

- Brown (½ yd) for Wreath Block, Tall Rose Block, Swirl Block 5" x 5", backing, binding
- Brown (¼ yd) for Wreath Block, Swirl Block 5" x 5"
- Brown (⅛ yd) for Wreath Block

Ecru (five different variations)

- Ecru (½ yd) for Swirl Block 5" x 5", Tall Rose Block, backing
- Three variations of Ecru (¼ yd each) for Wreath Block (spaghetti), Skinny Rose Block, Swirl Block 4" x 4", Swirl Block 5" x 5", Tall Rose Block
- Ecru (¼ yd) for Swirl Block 5" x 5"

Green (eight different variations)

- Five variations of green (¼ yd each) for Wreath Block, Swirl Block 4" x 4", Swirl Block 5" x 5", Tall Rose Block
- Green (½ yd) for Wreath Block, Swirl Block 4" x 4", Swirl Block 5" x 5", Tall Rose Block, backing
- Two variations of light green (¼ yd each) for Swirl Block 4" x 4", Skinny Rose Block

Purple (one variation)

- Purple (⅜ yd) for Wreath Block, Tall Rose Block, medallion on Swirl Block 5" x 5", backing

Red (one variation)

- Red (⅛ yd) for Wreath Block, Tall Rose Block

Rose (two different variations)

- Two variations of rose (¼ yd each) for Wreath Block, Skinny Rose Block, Swirl Block 4" x 4", Tall Rose Block

Rust (two different variations)

- Two variations of rust (¼ yd each) for Wreath Block, Tall Rose Block

NOTIONS:

Bugle bead: standard size, green

Low-loft or heirloom batting

Seed beads: brown silver lined; coral iris; crystal; matte plum; multimetallic gray; metallic olive; metallic silver

Silver beads: 6mm (4)

Silver rose beads: 8mm (2); 6mm (4)

WREATH BLOCK (A):

Note: Enlarge all patterns 200%.

1 Cut one 11½" x 12½" piece from green fabric for block background. Place **Pattern J** on page 29 on fold of rose fabric and cut one. Place **Pattern K** on page 29 on fold of rust fabric, and cut one. Cut 6¼" circle from purple fabric. Cut **Pattern M** on page 29 one left and one right from rust fabric. Cut 1" x 12½" strip from brown fabric. Cut 1"-wide bias from two fabrics, for total of 65". Cut six ⅝" x 12" spaghetti strips from ecru fabric, creating strips about 12" in length.

2 Piece together J and K, matching marks as shown in **Pattern Diagram**. Press seams open. Position "wreath" onto green block. Stitch in place ⅛" in from each outer edge. Position circle in place onto wreath. Stitch in place ⅛" in from outer edge. Position left and right Ms below wreath. Stitch in place ⅛" in from outer edges and along bottom edge.

Wreath Block

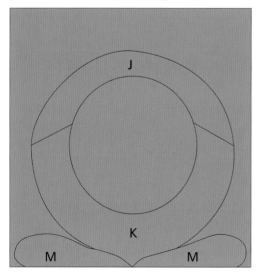

Pattern Diagram

3 Piece 1"-wide bias strips together end to end, alternating shades. Press in half, matching long edges. Align raw edges of bias with outer edge of M. Stitch bias to M, taking a ³⁄₁₆" seam allowance, curving bias while stitching to match curve of M. End bias just beyond where K and M meet. Repeat with opposite M piece. Trim ¹⁄₁₆" from seam allowance. Press bias toward outer edges of M pieces, covering all raw edges. Slip-stitch outer edge of bias in place, creating a finished edge. *Note: An alternative would be to machine-stitch bias in place.*

4 Beginning with bottom edge, stitch bias to outer wreath ring, following technique in Step 3. Beginning at top center, stitch bias to inner wreath edge in same manner.

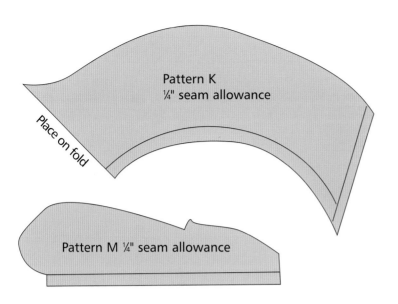

Pattern K
¼" seam allowance

Place on fold

Pattern M ¼" seam allowance

Fabric Variations

5 Piece two ⅝"-wide strips together. Fold one strip in half, wrong sides together, matching long edges. Stitch ⅛" from folded edge. Using loop turner, turn spaghetti right side out. Repeat with all pieces.

6 Position and pin spaghetti onto wreath as shown in **Wreath Block Diagram**. Knot spaghetti at inner and outer corners. Hand-stitch spaghetti in place.

Wreath Block Diagram

7 Stitch 12½" strip to bottom edge of block.

8 Refer to **Lotus Flower** on page 30 and **Lotus Leaf** on page 31. Using **Pattern N** and rust fabrics, make three five-petal folded flowers. Using eleven 3" squares and six green fabrics, make eleven leaves. *Note: Flowers and leaves will be appliquéd in place after quilting. Set flowers and leaves aside for now.*

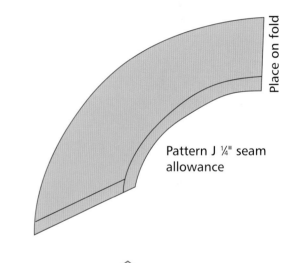

Place on fold

Pattern J ¼" seam allowance

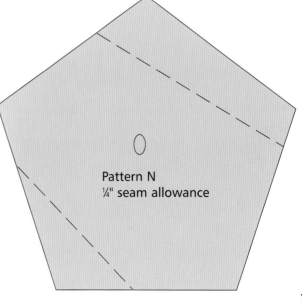

Pattern N
¼" seam allowance

29

LOTUS FLOWER:

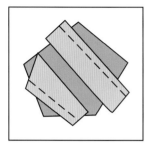 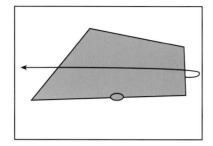 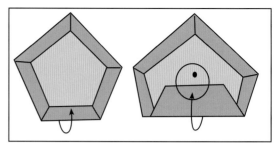

1 Using appropriate pattern, strip-piece coordinating fabrics on dotted lines. Press. Retrim to shape. Trim away excess under piece.

2 Press piece in half to find center. Make center on wrong side of fabric.

3 Press edges under ½". Fold bottom edge to center (wrong side is up). Stitch center of folded edge to center dot. Press and rotate counterclockwise.

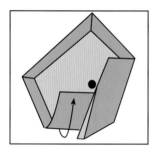 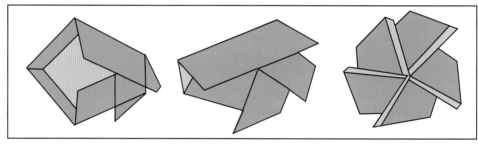

4 Fold bottom edge to center dot. Stitch at center as in Step 4. Press. Rotate counterclockwise.

5 Repeat with each edge: press, tack, rotate. Repeat for desired number of petals, according to number of sides of pattern.

6 For five-petal and six-petal blossoms, bring tip of one petal to center. Stitch tip. DO NOT PRESS.

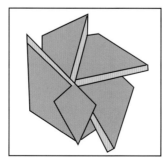 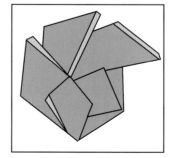

7 Repeat with each tip, overlapping petals.

This ornament was created using Pattern O on page 33 and instructions on opposite page. The petals were created using a 3" square for each petal of fabric and folded-square technique shown on pages 94–95. Working from bottom to top on a 2½" Styrofoam® ball, the petals and top flower have been secured to ball with pins hidden under the petal flaps. Beads were added for a finishing touch.

LOTUS LEAF:

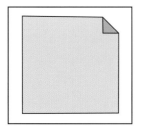

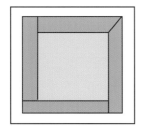

1 Press one corner up approximately ⅜".

2 Press all remaining edges up ¼".

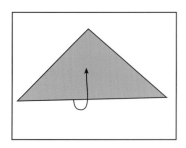

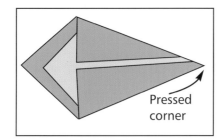

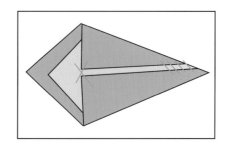

3 Fold in half to crease. Unfold.

4 Fold edge to center, press.

Pressed corner

5 Stitch here. Invisibly stitch narrow tip for ⅜". Turn over.

6 Fold up and tack tips together.

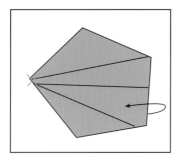

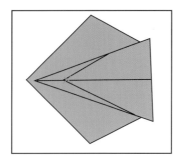

7 Bring two outer sides of touching folds of tip together. Stitch finger's width from tip for texture. *Note: Stuff back side for texture, if desired.*

SKINNY ROSE BLOCK (B):

1 Cut **Pattern F** on opposite page from lightest green fabric. Cut **Pattern G** on opposite page from darkest green fabric. Cut **Pattern H** on opposite page from pale green fabric. Cut 1"-wide bias strips from ecru fabric for a total of 15" for each block.

2 Refer to **Skinny Rose Block Diagram**. Overlap G onto F. Overlap H onto G/F. Stitch in place ⅛" in from design lines.

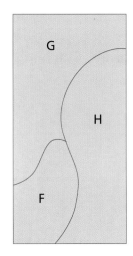

Skinny Rose
Block Diagram

3 Piece 1"-wide bias strips together. Press in half, matching long edges.

4 Refer to **Wreath Block (A)**, Step 3 on page 28. Stitch bias to G/F seam. Stitch bias to H seam.

5 Refer to **Lotus Flower** on page 30 and **Lotus Leaf** on page 31. Using **Pattern O** on opposite page and rose fabric, make one eight-petal folded flower. Using 3" square, make one leaf from aqua fabric. *Note: Flowers and leaf will be appliquéd in place after quilting.*

6 Repeat Steps 1–4 two times for three blocks. Stitch three B blocks together for Skinny Rose Block. Stitch **Wreath Block (A)** to **Skinny Rose Blocks (B)**.

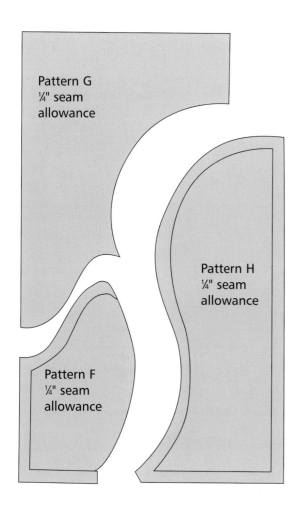

Pattern G
¼" seam
allowance

Pattern H
¼" seam
allowance

Pattern F
¼" seam
allowance

SWIRL BLOCK 5" X 5" (C):

1 Cut nine of **Pattern A**, cut nine left and nine right of **Pattern B**, and cut nine of **Pattern C** from brown fabric and ecru fabrics. Cut nine 1" x 10" bias strips from brown fabric. Cut ⅝"-wide bias strips from one ecru and one brown fabric, for a total of 80" altogether.

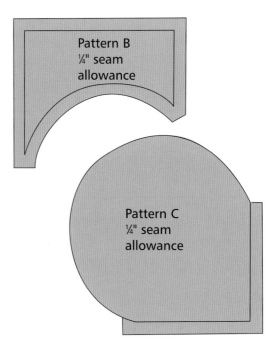

Pattern A
¼" seam
allowance

Pattern B
¼" seam
allowance

Pattern C
¼" seam
allowance

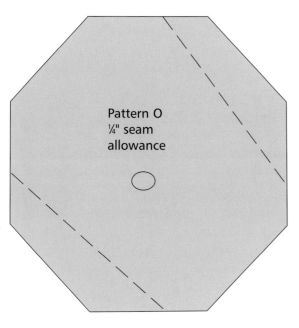

Pattern O
¼" seam
allowance

2 Stitch left and right Bs to A, matching marks. Overlap C onto A/B as shown in **Swirl Block Diagram**. Stitch in place ⅛" from curved edges.

3 Piece bias strips together. Press in half matching long edges.

4 Refer to **Wreath Block (A)**, Step 3 on page 28. Stitch bias to curved edge of C.

5 Stitch five blocks together for outermost row. Stitch four blocks together for bottom row.

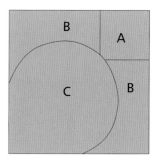

B

A

C

B

Swirl Block Diagram

6 Refer to **Lotus Flower** on page 30 and **Lotus Leaf** on page 31. Using **Pattern D** on opposite page and brown fabric, make one twelve-petal folded flower. Using six 3" squares and two green fabrics, make six leaves. *Note: Flowers and leaves will be appliquéd in place after quilting.*

7 Refer to **Wreath Block (A),** Step 5 on page 29. Make spaghetti strips. For lettering, knot strips together. Position and pin word CALM on first four blocks of bottom row. Hand-stitch spaghetti in place.

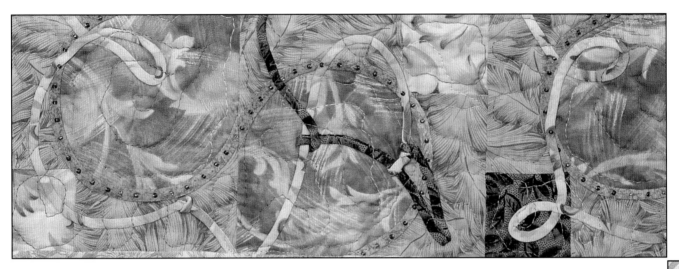

SWIRL BLOCK 4" X 4" (D):

1 Using **Patterns X, Y,** and **Z** on opposite page, two ecru fabrics, and green fabric, make four Swirl Blocks 4" x 4". Refer to **Swirl Block 5" x 5"** Steps 1–4 on page 33. Stitch four blocks together.

2 Refer to **Lotus Flower** on page 30 and **Lotus Leaf** on page 31. Using **Pattern D** on opposite page and rose fabric, make one twelve-petal folded flower. Using four 3" squares and four green fabrics, make four leaves. *Note: Flowers and leaves will be appliquéd in place after quilting.*

Tip:

The contrasting fabric strips added to the Lotus flowers (Patterns N, O, D, V, and U) help to make each folded petal more visible by drawing attention to itself through the contrast. The tone of the contrasting fabric should be different in a subtle way.

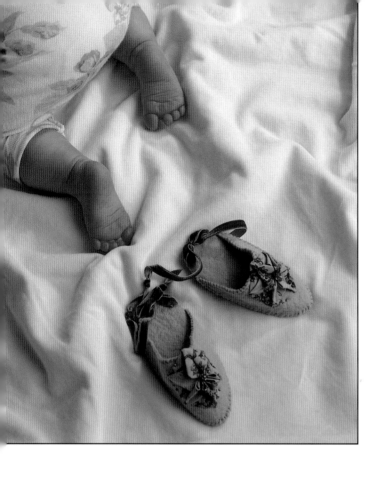

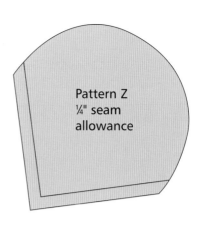

Pattern Z
¼" seam
allowance

Pattern Y
¼" seam allowance

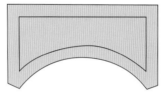

Pattern X
¼" seam
allowance

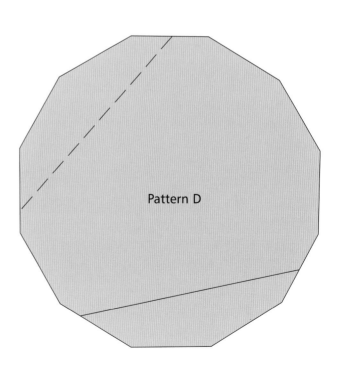

Pattern D

TALL ROSE BLOCK (E):

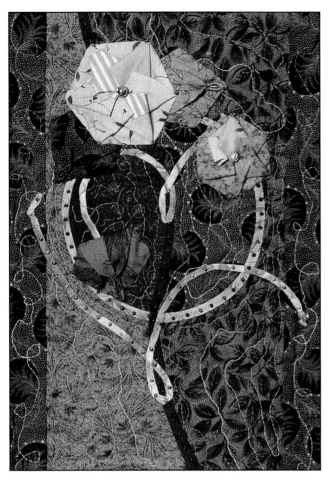

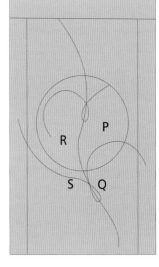

Tall Rose Block Diagram

4 Refer to **Wreath Block (A)**, Step 5 on page 29 Make spaghetti strips. Position and pin in place on block as shown in **Tall Rose Block Diagram**. Hand-stitch spaghetti in place.

5 Refer to **Lotus Flower** on page 30 and **Lotus Leaf** on page 31. Using **Pattern U** on opposite page and rose fabric, make one six-petal folded flower. Using **Pattern V** on opposite page and rose fabric, make smaller six-petal folded flower. Using three 3" squares from green fabric, make leaves. *Note: Flowers and leaves will be appliquéd in place after quilting.*

6 Stitch **Swirl Block (D)** to top edge of **Tall Rose Block (E)**.

7 Stitch all blocks together as shown in **Lotus Quilt Diagram**.

1 Cut **Pattern P** on opposite page from green fabric. Cut **Pattern Q** on opposite page from rust fabric. Cut **Pattern R** on opposite page from from green fabric. Cut **Pattern S** on opposite page from red fabric. Cut two of **Pattern T** on opposite page from purple fabric. Cut 1" x 15" bias strip from brown fabric and 1" x 18" bias strip from ecru fabric. Cut ⅝" x 30" spaghetti strip from ecru fabric. *Note: Bias is not pieced together.*

2 Overlap R onto P and overlap S onto Q. Overlap S/Q onto R/P. Stitch pieces in place ⅛" from design lines.

3 Refer to **Wreath Block (A)**, Step 3 on page 28. Beginning at center top, stitch ecru bias to circle outer edge. Stitch brown bias to remaining curved seam line. Stitch T to either side of block.

Lotus Quilt Diagram

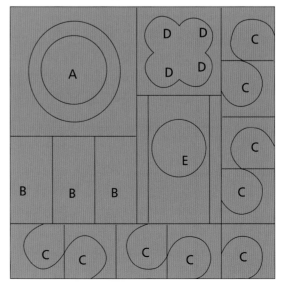

BORDER & BACKING:

1. Cut four 1½" strips from blue/ecru fabric for border. Stitch strips to sides. Stitch strips to top and bottom.

2. Cut sixteen 6½" squares from backing fabrics. Piece squares together, four per row, creating four rows.

3. Layer backing, batting, and quilt top. Pin-baste together. Free-motion machine-quilt.

4. Cut four 1½"-wide strips from brown fabric. Bind quilt with brown strips. Appliqué flowers and leaves in place on each block.

5. Stitch large beads to flower centers and one seed bead at each outer corner. Stitch one bugle bead within each leaf tip. Stitch seed beads onto bias and spaghetti to accent design. Space beads ¼" apart, using bead shades in a random fashion.

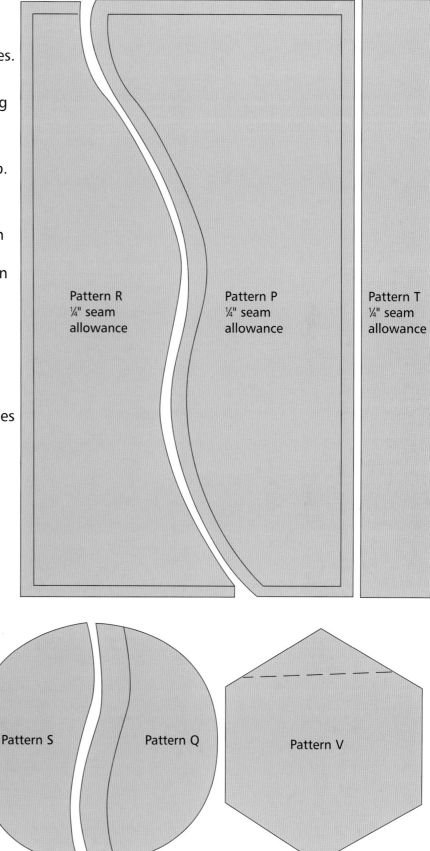

Pattern R
¼" seam
allowance

Pattern P
¼" seam
allowance

Pattern T
¼" seam
allowance

Pattern U

Pattern S

Pattern Q

Pattern V

WHERE THE FROG
LEAPS, THE SNAIL GOES
SLOWLY; BOTH ARRIVE.

SKETCHBOOK QUILT

FABRICS:

Note: All fabrics are 42"–45" wide.

Black/white (one variation)
- Black/white (3¾" x 7") for one frog

Brick (one variation)
- Brick (⅛ yd) for Little Leaf Block

Brown (two different variations)
- Brown (⅜ yd) for Snail Block, Frog Block, border
- Brown (¼ yd) for Snail Block, branches

Continued on page 40.

Continued from page 39.

Burgundy (three different variations)

- Two variations of burgundy (⅜ yd each) for Pinwheel Block, Frog Block, Double Triangles Block, backing, border

Coral (one variation)

- Coral (¼ yd) for Yankee Puzzle with Spokes, Snail Block

Green (nine different variations)

- Two variations of green (¼ yd each) for large, little, and wide leaves, Pinwheel Block
- Green (⅜ yd) for large and little leaves, backing
- Two variations of green (¼ yd each) for large, little, and wide Leaves, Pinwheel Block, Snail Block
- Three variations of green (¼ yd each) for large and wide leaves, Snail Block, Pinwheel Block
- Green (⅜ yd) for Pinwheel Block, backing

Lavender/blue (five different variations)

- Five different variations of lavender/blue (¼ yd each) for Yankee Puzzle with Spokes Block, Pinwheel Block, Snail Block, border

Neutral (four different variations)

- Neutral with leaf imprint (½ yd) for backing, Snail Block, Upside-down Triangle Block, Frog Block, Single Triangle Block, Pinwheel Block
- Three variations of neutral (¼ yd each) for Snail Block, Upside-down Triangle Block, Frog Block, Leaf Block, Single Triangle Block, Pinwheel Block

Orange/gold (one variation)

- Orange/gold (¼ yd) for Frog Block, Double Triangle Block

Fabric Variations

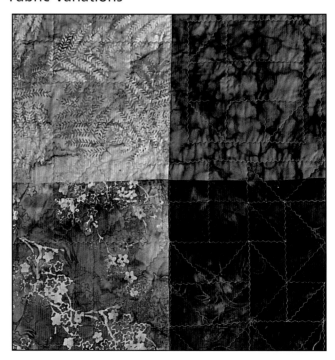

YANKEE PUZZLE WITH SPOKES BLOCK (A):

Note: Enlarge all patterns 200%.

1 Cut ten 4" squares from Lavender/ blue fabrics. Cut each square diagonally in half twice.

2 Using **Pattern I**, cut forty spokes from coral fabrics.

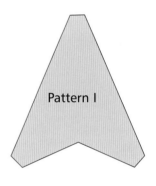

3 Press spoke in half. Press top edge over. Insert into seam between triangles. Repeat thirty-nine times for forty spokes.

4 Assemble ten Yankee Puzzle Blocks with Spokes Blocks by stitching cut edge of spoke into seam while stitching block together.

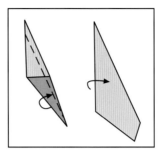

Pattern I

PINWHEEL BLOCK (B):

1 Cut four 4" squares from lavender/blue fabrics. Cut thirteen 4" squares from green fabrics. Cut each square in half twice.

2 Cut sixteen 2½" squares from lavender/blue fabrics. Cut fifty-two 2½" squares from green fabrics.

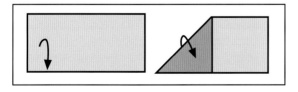

3 Press 2½" squares in half.

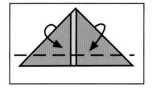

4 Press corners down, creating triangle.

5 Assemble seventeen Pinwheel Blocks by stitching cut edge of triangle into seam while stitching block together.

UPSIDE-DOWN TRIANGLE BLOCK (C):

1 Cut sixteen 2½" x 4½" rectangles from neutral fabrics. Cut sixteen 4" squares from neutral fabrics.

2 Press 4" squares in half.

3 Press corners down, creating triangle.

4 Assemble four Upside-down Triangle Blocks by stitching cut edge of triangle into seam while stitching block together.

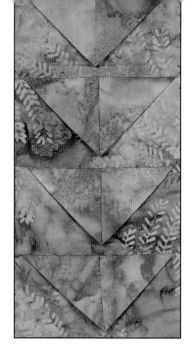

SINGLE TRIANGLE BLOCK (G):

1 Cut six 2½" x 4½" rectangles from neutral fabrics. Cut six 4" squares from neutral fabrics.

2 Press 4" squares in half.

3 Press corners down, creating triangle.

4 Assemble six Single Triangle Blocks by stitching cut edge of triangle onto one edge.

DOUBLE TRIANGLE BLOCK (H):

1 Cut eight 2½" x 4½" rectangles from burgundy fabric and orange fabric. Cut eight 4" squares from burgundy and orange fabrics.

2 Press 4" squares in half.

3 Press corners down, creating triangle.

4 Assemble four Double Triangle Blocks by stitching one cut edge of triangle onto one edge and one into seam while stitching block together.

SNAIL BLOCK (D):

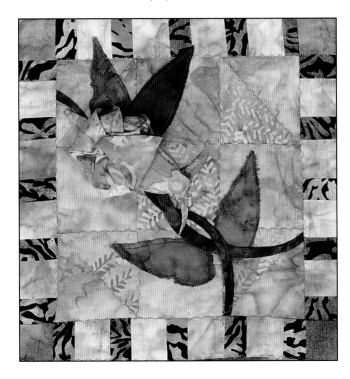

5 For each block, cut one 1" x 32" strip from brown fabric. Cut one 1⅜" x 26" strip from neutral fabric. Stitch strips together lengthwise. Cut strip into 1½" pieces. Stitch four pieces together for each side, adding another 1" x 1½" piece from remaining brown strip at the appropriate end.

6 Using **Pattern C** and neutral fabrics, cut twelve corner squares for block corners. Stitch strips to each block side, adding corners to appropriate ends.

1 Cut twenty-four of **Pattern A** and fifteen of **Pattern B** from neutral fabrics for Snail Block center.

2 Assemble one block as shown in **Snail Block Diagram**. Repeat two more times.

3 Cut 1" x 20" bias strips from brown fabric for branches. Stitch bias and turn right side out. Position bias loosely onto center of block. Stitch bias ends in place along sides of block.

Snail Block Diagram

4 Using **Pattern D** and green fabrics, cut three or four small leaves. Machine-stitch leaves in place among branches, placing stitches ⅛" in from cut edges. Run fingernail along cut edges, fraying leaves slightly.

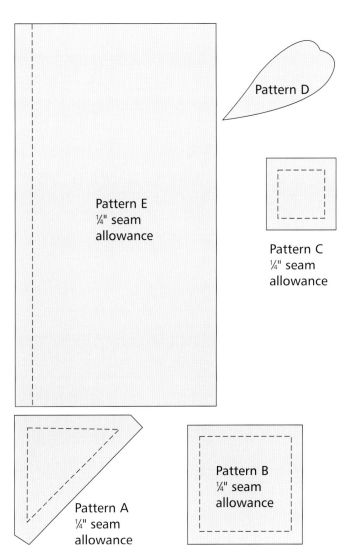

Snail:

Using two different fabrics for each snail, make three snails, following Steps 1–23 below and on pages 45–46. *Note: Snails are appliquéd in place after quilt has been assembled and machine-quilted.*

1 Piece together two of **Pattern E** on page 43. Press seam open. Clip bulk at center.

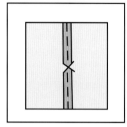

2 With wrong side up, press on dashed lines. Turn over.

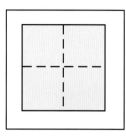

3 With right side up, press diagonally.

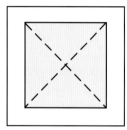

4 Fold and press.

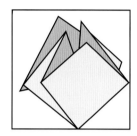

5 Bring right corner to center. Flatten or press.

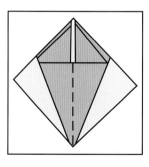

6 Fold small triangle over to right. Press.

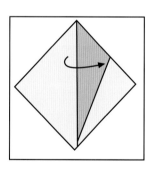

7 Bring left corner to center. Press.

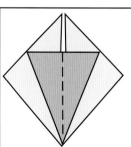

8 Fold small triangle to left. Press. Turn over.

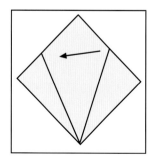

9 Repeat Steps 5–8 on page 44.

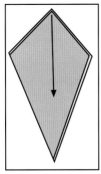

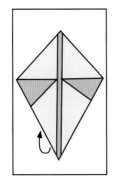

10 Bring top point down to meet bottom point. Press tip up ¼" for clean finish.

11 Fold bottom tip up. Press.

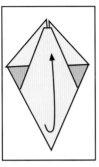

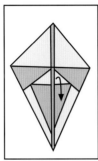

12 Fold upper tip down, just above center.

13 Fold right edge over to center and flatten. Press. Repeat with left edge.

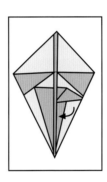

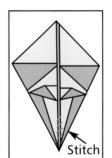

Stitch

14 Stitch for snail's tail.

15 Fold right edge over to left, hiding tail.

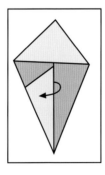

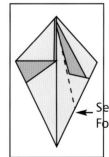

Second Fold Line

16 Fold upper-right edge over three times. Fold over to left.

17 Fold larger right edge over to left.

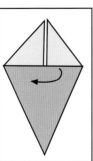

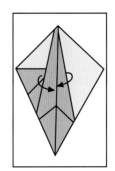

18 Fold upper-left and right edges over three times, as in Step 16.

19 Fold top four layers to right. Repeat Steps 16–18 on page 45 with left side.

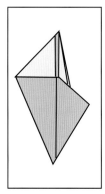

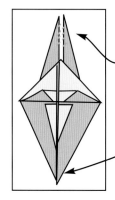

20 Fold top three layers to left. Hand-stitch antennae. Spray starch tips under tail.

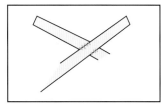

21 Crisscross antennae and stitch overlap.

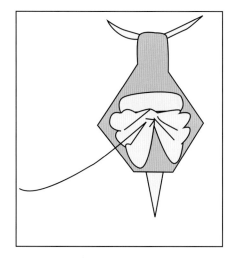

23 Fold up bottom point. Pin shell folds to outer triangles. Stitch in place. Twist tip, then stitch to hold.

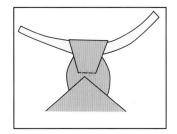

22 Fold top tip over crossed antennae, tucking under raw edge. Stitch. Turn over.

LEAF BLOCK (E):

1 Cut forty of **Pattern A** on page 43 and cut twenty of **Pattern G** from neutral fabrics.

2 Assemble by stitching two As to each G, for rectangle. Stitch four rectangles together for Leaf Block. Repeat four times.

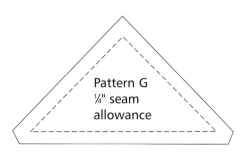

Pattern G
¼" seam allowance

Tall Leaf:

Using **Pattern F** and two green fabrics, make five leaves, following Steps 1–7 below. *Note: Leaves are appliquéd in place after quilt has been assembled and machine-quilted.*

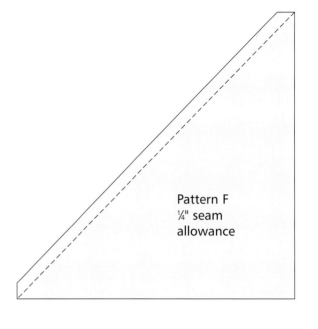

Pattern F
¼" seam
allowance

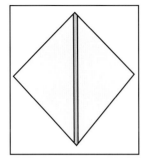

1 Piece together two of appropriate patterns. Seam triangles. Press seam open.

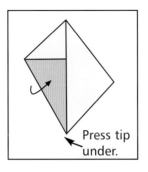

Press tip under.

2 Wrong side up. Press tip under ¼". Press both sides to center.

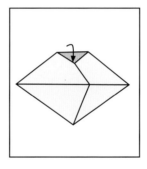

Press tip under.

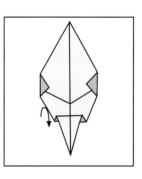

3 Press tip under ¼". Press both top edges to center.

4 Press side points over ½".

5 Press bottom point up and back down.

6 Fold tip ends together. Stitch. Press stem over and flatten on both sides.

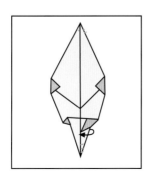

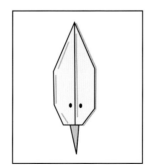

7 Stitch together.

LITTLE LEAF ROW (I):

1 Cut five 3½" x 4½" pieces from brick fabric.

2 Using **Pattern O** and two green fabrics, make five leaves, following Steps 1–7 on page 47. *Note: Leaves are appliquéd in place after quilt has been assembled and machine quilted.*

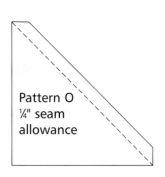

Pattern O
¼" seam
allowance

FROG BLOCK (F):

1 Cut forty-eight of **Pattern A** on page 43 and cut twenty-four of **Pattern G** on page 46 from neutral fabrics.

2 Assemble by stitching two As to each G, for rectangle. Stitch remaining As together and remaining Gs together. Assemble block as shown in **Frog Block Diagram**. Repeat three times for four blocks.

3 Using **Pattern L** and two different green fabrics, make three leaves, following folding Steps 1–7 on page 47. *Note: Leaves are appliquéd in place after quilt has been assembled and machine-quilted.*

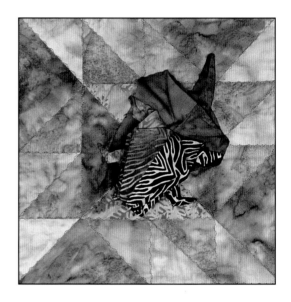

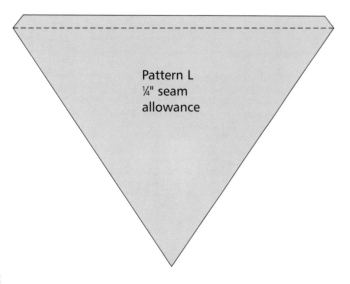

Pattern L
¼" seam
allowance

Frog Block Diagram

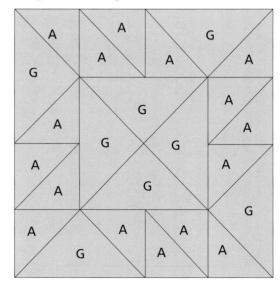

Frog:

Using two different fabrics for each frog, make three Frogs following Steps 1–8 below. *Note: Frogs are appliquéd in place after quilt has been assembled and machine-quilted.*

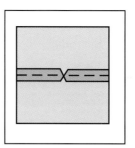

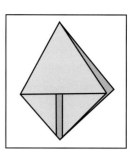

1 Cut two 3¾" x 7" pieces. Seam pieces. Press seam open. Clip block at center.

2 Fold same as Snail, Steps 2–9 on pages 44–45.

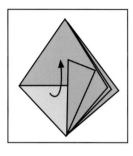

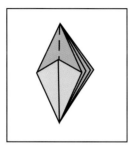

3 Pull up straight edge while folding in sides. Flatten. Repeat for remaining three flaps.

4 Spray with starch.

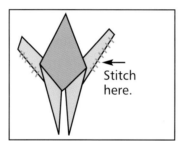

Stitch here.

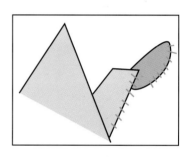

5 Pull up and out on upper legs from back layers. Fold tip under ¼". Stitch as indicated above.

6 Fold upper leg down, up, then tack.

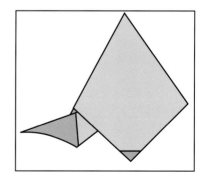

7 Pull out lower legs from front layers. Stitch as indicated.

8 Squish in upper tip. Stuff tip lightly. Fold front and back tips under ¼". Tack tips together.

BORDER & BACKING:

1 Stitch blocks together first within their numerical sequence then together as larger pieces as shown in **Sketch Book Quilt Diagram**.

2 Cut 1¾"-wide strips from three lavender fabrics, two burgundy fabrics, and one green fabric. Piece strips together, then stitch onto sides, top, and bottom of quilt.

3 Machine-quilt as desired. Bind with brown fabric.

4 Appliqué all leaves, snails, and frogs in place.

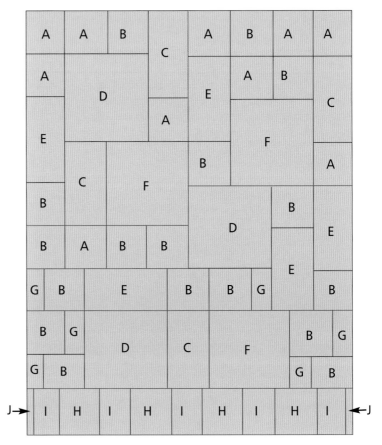

Sketch Book Quilt Diagram

Sketch Book Quilt Legend

A=Yankee Puzzle with Spokes

B=Pinwheel

C=Upside-down Triangle

D=Snail

E=Leaf

F=Frog

G=Single Triangle

H=Double Triangle

I=Little Leaf

J=extra pieces for length

This unique shadow box was created using the origami frog from page 49 and the origami tall leaf on page 47. These figures are ornately displayed on coordinating fabric pieced background. The shadow box frame has been covered with fabric to add the finishing touch.

CAT QUILT

Assorted colors (seventeen variations)

- Three assorted colors (8" square each) for cats
- Seven assorted colors (8" square each) for butterflies
- Seven assorted colors (4" square each) for trees

Olive green (three variations)

- Olive green (⅛ yd) for center strip
- Olive green (1 yd) for backing/border
- Olive green barkcloth (⅝ yd) for background

NOTIONS:

Assorted beads (6)

Bugle beads (3)

Embroidery flosses: brown; green

Embroidery needle

Quilt batting (½ yd)

NATURE SHINES THROUGH THE EYES OF A CAT.

CAT QUILT:

1 Cut 20¼" x 30" piece from barkcloth. Cut 5" x 30" piece from olive green cotton. Cut 5" x 30" piece from batting.

2 With batting piece underneath olive green piece, appliqué cotton fabric to barkcloth, placing strip 5" up from one 30" side. Turn edges under ¼" while appliquéing in place.

Cat:

Using three assorted fabrics, make three cats, following Steps 1–11 below and on page 55.

1 Fold corners of 8" square to center. Trim away fabric on dotted lines.

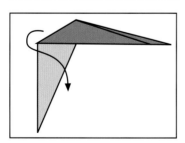

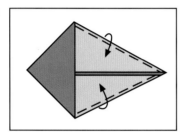

2 Fold left edge to center. Repeat for right edge.

3 Fold trimmed edges to center.

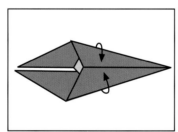

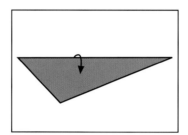

4 Fold in half.

5 On left side, fold inside reverse fold down.

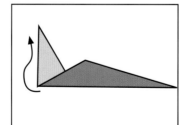

6 Turn up and over. Fold up with inside-reverse fold. Turn over.

7 Flatten top point.

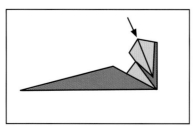

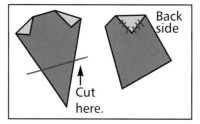

Back side

Cut here.

8 Fold upper points down for ears. Fold center point to back. Tack. Cut off in front.

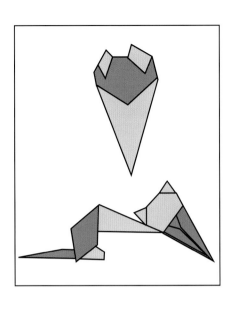

9 Fold cut-off ends under. Tack on underside. *Note: This is the face.*

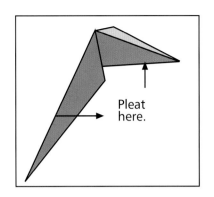

Pleat here.

10 Fold outside-reverse on dash for tail.

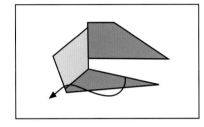

11 Fold inside-reverse, then out for tail.

Tree:

Using three assorted fabrics, make seven trees, following Steps 1–6 below.

1 Fold corners of 4" square to center.

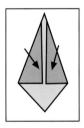

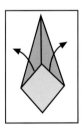

2 Fold inner corners under. Open out and turn over.

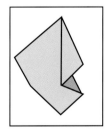

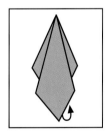

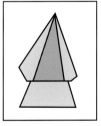

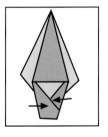

3 Pleat-crease to center on both sides. Turn over.

4 Press bottom point under.

5 Place contrasting fabric strip under bottom. Wrap strip around "trunk" then pleat.

6 Fold trunk ends over. Turn over to see right side of tree.

55

Butterfly:

Using three assorted fabrics, make seven butterflies, following Steps 1–5 below.

  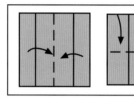

1 Press all edges of 8" square under ¼". Crease diagonally and squarely.

2 Fold outer edge to center in both directions. Keep folded.

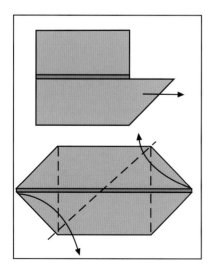 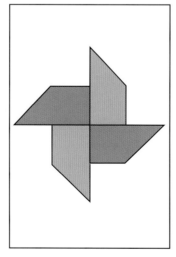 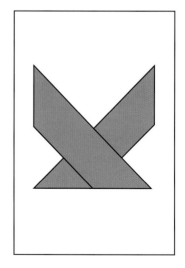

3 Pull out all four corners from inside.

4 Fold upper right up and lower left down.

5 Fold diagonally in half.

FINISHING:

1 Appliqué cats, trees, and butterflies onto fabric at top and bottom edges of appliquéd strip.

2 Stitch assorted beads on cats for eyes. Stitch bugle beads on cats for nose. Using six strands of brown embroidery floss, pull floss in one side and out other side of cat's face for whiskers. Trim to desired length. Separate strands into groups of three. Tie and knot close to face.

3 For lettering, using pencil, draw lettering onto strip. Backstitch lettering onto quilt with green embroidery floss.

4 Bind quilt as desired.

Lettering

Tips:

There are two key challenges in fabric origami: how to finish the raw edges (and in which step to prepare for finishing) and how to deal with the fabric's bulk once folded. For each folded fabric shape, these challenges have been resolved for you in the step-by-step folding directions. If you have never done origami or if it's been a while since you have folded origami shapes, practice the steps with paper before moving on to fabric. You will find the fabric to be much more cooperative than paper. When you are ready to experiment with new shapes not offered in this book, remember to resolve these two challenges of finishing the raw edges and eliminating bulk.

COME PLAY WITH ME QUILT

THERE ARE TWO LASTING
BEQUESTS WE CAN GIVE OUR
CHILDREN: ONE IS ROOTS.
THE OTHER IS WINGS.

FABRICS:

Note: All fabrics are 42"–45" wide.

Blue (sixteen different variations)

- Blue (¼ yd) for Sunrise Block, Fan Mill Pocket Block's lining
- Blue (½ yd) for Flying Kites Block, Sunrise Block, Rubber Duckie Block, Fan Mill Pocket Block, Sea Gull Block
- Two variations of blue (⅛ yd each) for Flying Kites Block
- Four variations of blue (⅛ yd each) for Fan Mill Pocket Block
- Blue (¼ yd) for Fan Mill Pocket Block
- Blue (¼ yd) for Flying Kites Block, below Sunrise Block, Sea Gull Block, binding
- Blue polka-dotted (½ yd) for Flying Kites Block, Fan Mill Pocket Block's binding, Sea Gull Block
- Three variations of blue (⅛ yd each) for Flying Kites Block, Sea Gull Block
- Two variations of blue (⅛ yd each) for Sea Gull Block

Ecru (four different variations)

- Ecru (½ yd) for Flying Kites Block, Sunrise Block, backing
- Three variations of ecru (⅛ yd each) for Flying Kites Block

Green (three variations)

- Green (⅛ yd) for Flying Kites Block
- Green (½ yd) for Fan Mill Pocket Block's background
- Green (⅛ yd) for Chubby Guys

Gold (five different variations)

- Three variations of gold (½ yd each) for Sunrise Block, Flying Kites Block, Rubber Duckie Block, Sea Gull Block, backing
- Gold (½ yd) for Sunrise Block, Flying Kites Block, backing
- Gold (⅛ yd) for Rubber Duckie Block

Lavender (two variations)

- Lavender (⅛ yd) for Flying Kites Block, Sea Gull Block
- Lavender (¼ yd) for Flying Kites Block, sashing

Mauve (one variation)

- Mauve (¼ yd) for seal

Orange (three variations)

- Orange (¼ yd) for Sunrise Block, Flying Kites Block, Sea Gull Block
- Two variations of Orange (⅛ yd each) for Flying Kites Block, Chubby Guys' heads, Rubber Duckies Block

Peach (one variation)

- Peach (⅛ yd) for Sea Gull Block

Sage (one variation)

- Sage (½ yd) for Sea Gull Block, border

Sage/lavender (one variation)

- Sage/lavender (½ yd) for Sea Gull Block

Continued on opposite page.

White prints (four variations)

- Two variations of white prints (⅛ yd each) for Flying Kites Block
- White with polka dots (¼ yd) for Flying Kites Block, Rubber Duckie Block
- Natural white broadcloth (½ yd) for background

Note: Full quilt diagram shown on page 75.

NOTIONS:

Embroidery floss: brown
Low-loft or heirloom batting

SUNRISE BLOCK (A):

Note: Enlarge all patterns 200%.

1 Cut broadcloth 6" x 26". Using pencil, trace **Sunrise Pattern** onto broadcloth. Refer to Foundation Piecing on page 14. Beginning at left edge, foundation-piece strips of sky/sunlight onto broadcloth, following numerical sequence. Cut 5" circle in half for sun and pin in place.

2 Cut 1" x 9" bias strip from orange fabric. Fold and press bias in half, lengthwise. Align raw edge of bias with raw edge of sun, right sides together. Stitch, taking ¼" seam allowance. Trim seam to ⅛". Fold bias over, covering raw edge of bias/sun. Hand-stitch in place. Trim block to 5½" x 25½".

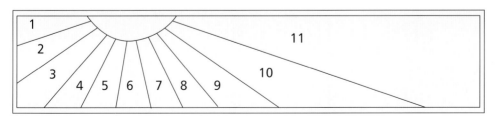

Sunrise Pattern

Seal:

Using mauve fabric, make one seal, following Steps 1–14 below and on page 63.

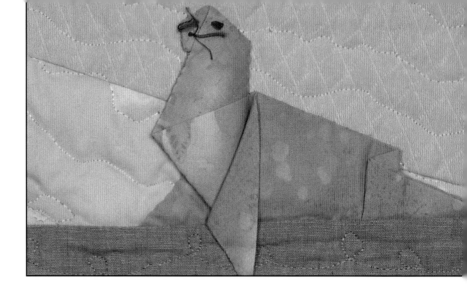

1 Cut 8" square from mauve fabric. Turn on point. Press corners inward.

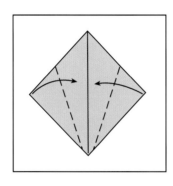

2 Turn over.

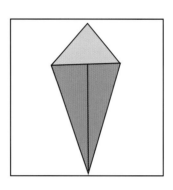

3 Fold in half and crease.

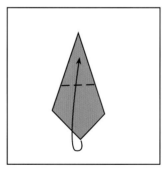

4 Open out and press down. Do both sides.

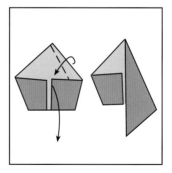

5 Fold top layer down.

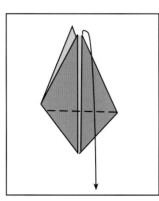

6 Press and turn over.

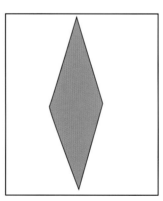

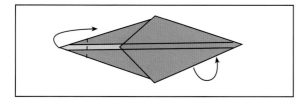 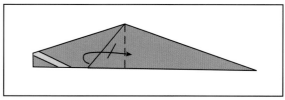

7 Press point in 1¼". Fold in half, raw edges at bottom. Press.

8 Press top flap over and unfold.

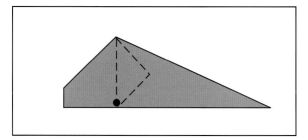 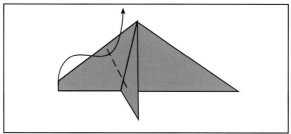

9 Clip to dot with scissors (¼" in from raw edges). Refold and press.

10 Fold left end inward and up at dotted line. Press.

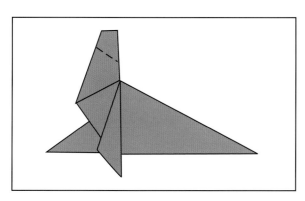 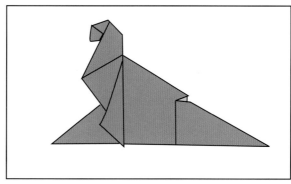

11 Fold top inward and down on dotted line. Press.

12 Pleat and press.

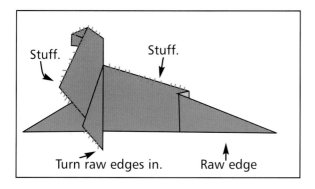

Stuff.

Stuff.

Turn raw edges in.

Raw edge

13 Lightly stuff seal. Stitch closed. Lightly stuff body. Stitch closed. Turn raw edges in at tip of fin. Pin seal in place on left side of **Sunrise Block**.

14 Cut 1½" x 25½" strip from blue fabric. Stitch to bottom of **Sunrise Block**, catching in raw edges of seal when sewing. Do not catch front fin in seam.

FLYING KITES BLOCK (B):

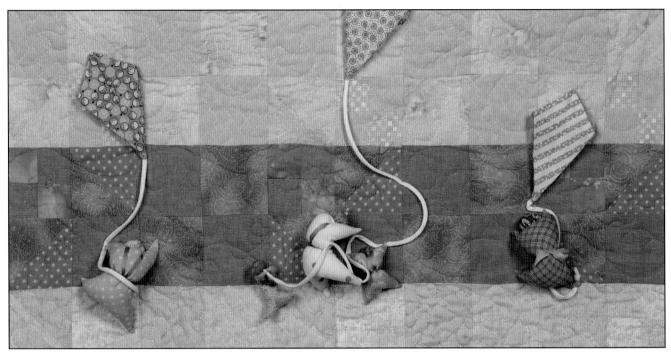

1 Cut twenty-two 3" squares from two blue fabrics. Cut five 3" squares from ecru fabric.

2 Cut twenty-four of **Pattern B** from two blue fabrics. Cut twelve of **Pattern B** from ecru fabric.

3 Stitch two Bs of same blue fabric together, forming 3" square. Repeat eight times for nine squares from blue fabrics and ecru fabrics.

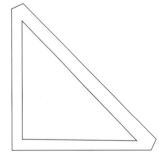

Pattern B
¼" seam allowance

4 Stitch four 1½" blocks together, forming 3" square. Repeat eight times for nine squares from blue fabrics and ecru fabrics.

5 Stitch four 3" squares together, forming one block. Repeat three times for four blue blocks.

6 Stitch two B squares, one 3" square, and one square from Step 5 of same color group together, forming block. Repeat five times for six blocks.

7 Alternately, stitch five of each of blue assembled blocks of same color group together in a strip. Repeat for second blue group. Stitch bottom of blue strip to top edge of second blue strip.

8 Alternately, stitch ecru squares together into strip below. Stitch bottom of second blue strip to top edge of ecru strip for **Flying Kite Block**.

Chubby Guy:

Using 4" x 4½" piece, and different fabrics for each chubby guy, make four chubby guys, following Steps 1–9 below and on page 66. *Note: Three chubby guys are appliquéd in place after quilt has been assembled and machine-quilted. The remaining chubby guy will be placed in a Fan Mill Pocket.*

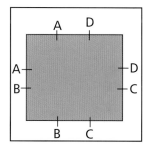

1 Measure 1½" from each corner.

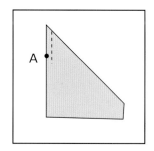

2 Fold one corner, matching As. Stitch to corner.

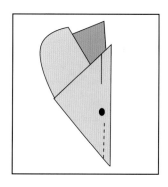

3 Fold and match Bs. Stitch to corner.

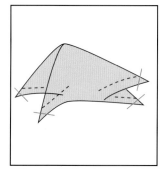

4 Repeat with remaining corners. Clip corners. Turn right side out.

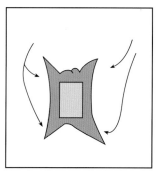

5 Stuff corners.

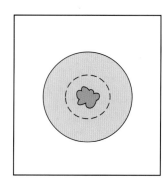

6 Cut 3" circle. Gather-stitch on dotted line. Place stuffing in center.

7 Pull stitches tightly, enclosing fabric stuffing. Wrap thread three times tightly around fabric. Knot.

8 Stitch head to body.

9 Finish stuffing body. Stitch opening closed.

Toddler:

Using 2½" x 3" piece and different fabrics for each toddler, make two toddlers, following Steps 1–9 on page 65 and above (except use 2½" circle for Step 6). *Note: Toddlers are appliquéd in place after quilt has been assembled and machine-quilted.*

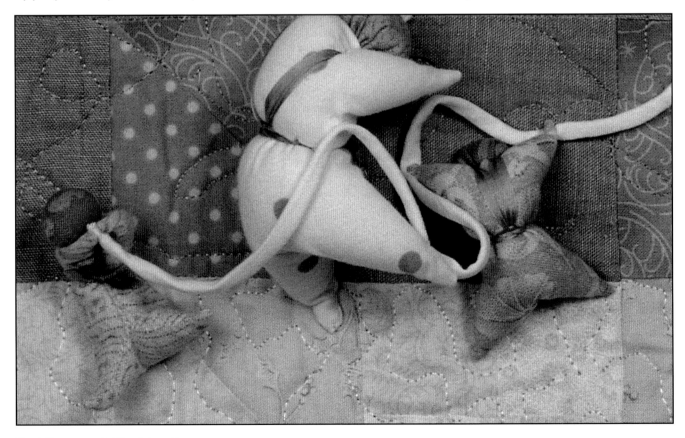

Toddlers and Chubby Guy

Kite Block

Kite:

Using two 3½" x 6½" pieces from two different fabrics for each kite, make three kites, following Steps 1–10 below and page 68. *Note: Kites are appliquéd in place after quilt has been assembled and machine-quilted.*

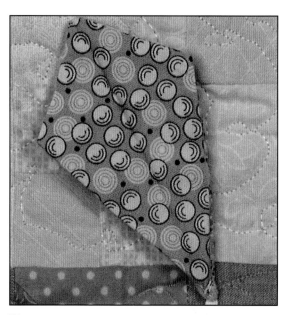

Kite

1 Stitch fabric with ¼" seam allowance. Cut notch at center of seam. Press seam open.

2 Trim 1" away from opposite corners. Trim.

3 Press all edges under ¼".

4 Crease.

5 With wrong side up, turn on end with trimmed corners at top and bottom. Fold down, pushing sides in at creases to form square.

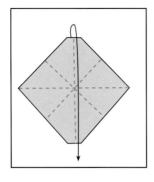

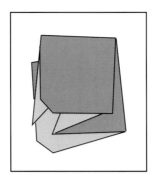

6 Push flat. Press, keeping it square.

7 Press top layer to center.

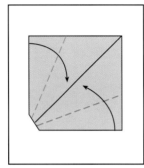

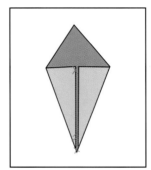

8 Stitch tip and top.

9 Turn over and repeat Steps 7–8.

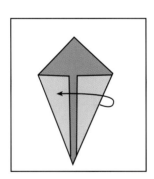

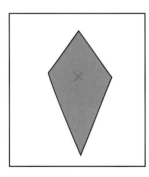

10 Fold over top layer to left on both sides and tack.

Kite Strings:

1 Cut three ⅝" x 12" bias strips from broadcloth. Stitch bias, turn right side out. Set aside. *Note: Kites strings are appliquéd in place after quilt has been assembled and machine-quilted.*

2 Stitch sky edge of **Flying Kites Block** to blue strip on bottom edge of **Sunrise Block**.

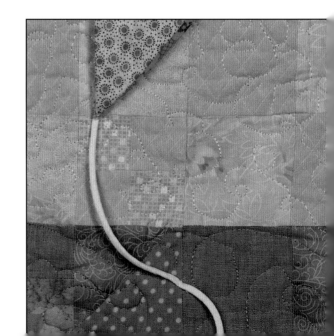

RUBBER DUCKIE BLOCK (C):

1. Cut four 4½" x 5½" pieces from blue fabric. Cut eight 2" x 6" pieces from white polka-dotted fabric.

2. Using water-soluble marker and 6" pieces, draw scallops as desired onto wrong sides of four of 6" pieces. Pin marked pieces to remaining 2" x 6" pieces with right sides together. Stitch directly onto traced lines. Trim seam to ⅛". Clip curves. Edge-press and turn right side out. Press. Pin onto 5½" pieces.

Rubber Duckie:

Using 6" squares from different fabrics for each rubber duckie, make four rubber duckies, following Steps 1–12 below and on page 70.

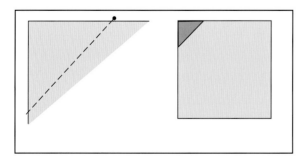 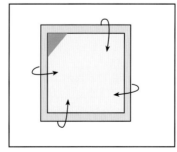 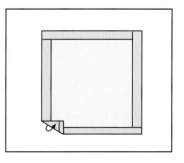

1. Stitch a scrap of orange fabric to corner on 1½" marks. Trim seam to ⅛". Press seam toward corner.

2. Press all edges under ¼".

3. Press contrast corner up, leaving ¼" of contrast fabric showing on right side.

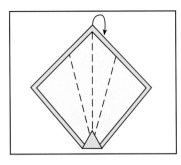

4 Crease on dotted lines, wrong edges up, open back out.

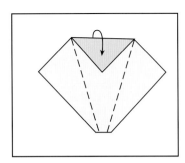

5 Fold top edge down to side creases. Press.

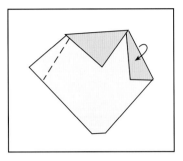

6 Fold top left and right corners down 1". Press.

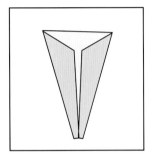

7 Fold outer edges to center. Press.

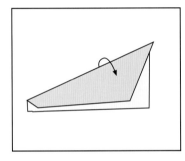

8 Fold in half. Press.

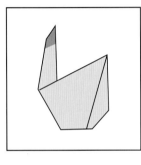

9 Fold left edge back and up. Pin.

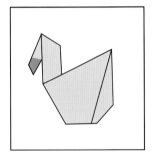

10 Fold top corner back and down. Pin.

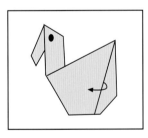

11 Fold bottom right corner under.

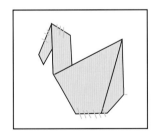

12 Hand-stitch beak, head, chest, and tail closed. Stuff front wing.

Sash:

1 Pin rubber duckies in place under scalloped water. Appliqué.

2 Cut five 1½" x 4½" strips from lavender fabric. Sash **Rubber Duckie Blocks** together. Stitch top of **Rubber Duckie Block** to bottom edge of **Flying Kites Block**.

FAN MILL POCKET BLOCK (D):

1 Cut twenty of **Pattern B** on page 64, cut five of **Pattern L**, and five reverse of **Pattern L** from blue fabric variations.

2 Stitch four Bs, one L, and one reverse L together as shown in **Fan Mill Pocket Diagram** for block. Repeat four times for five blocks. Stitch five blocks together.

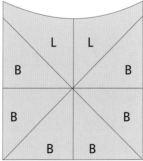

Fan Mill Pocket Diagram

3 Cut 5" x 26" piece from blue for Fan Mill Pocket Block's lining. Place wrong side up. Place quilt batting on top of fabric. Pin-baste **Fan Mill Pocket Block** over quilt batting. Machine quilt. Trim batting and blue fabric to match scallops.

4 Cut 1¼" x 27" bias strip from blue polka-dotted fabric for Fan Mill Pocket Block's binding. Bind scalloped pocket edges with bias.

5 Cut 8" x 25½" strip from green fabric for Fan Mill Pocket's background. Pin back side of quilted pocket block to right side of green strip, aligning bottom and side edges. Stitch in place along seams between **Fan Mill Pocket Blocks** at ends and bottom. Stitch top edge of **Fan Mill Pocket Block** to bottom edge of **Rubber Duckie Block**.

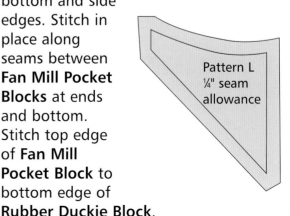

Pattern L
¼" seam allowance

71

SEA GULL BLOCK (E):

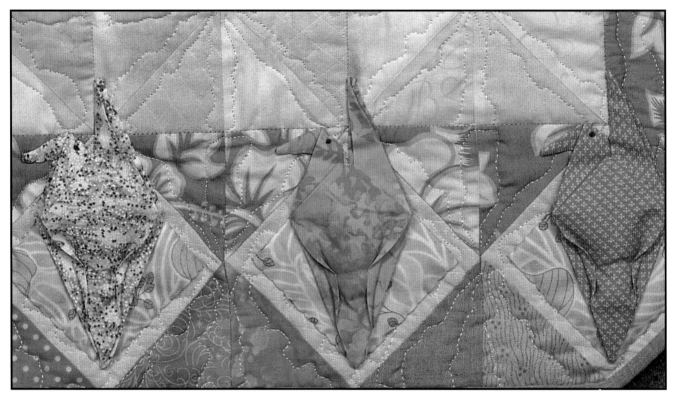

1 Cut six 4" squares from blue fabrics, cut ten of **Pattern B** on page 64 from sage fabric, and cut ten of **Pattern B** from blue fabrics.

2 Stitch two sage Bs, 4" square, and two blue Bs together as shown in **Sea Gull Block Diagram** for block. Repeat three times for four blocks.

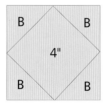

Sea Gull Block Diagram

3 Stitch remaining sage B, 4" square, and blue B together for half block. Repeat for two blocks.

4 Stitch blocks together, placing half blocks on each end. Stitch top edge of **Sea Gull Block** to bottom edge of **Fan Mill Pocket Block**.

Sea Gull:

Cut six 4¼" x 8" pieces from same fabric and cut six 4½" x 8" pieces from different fabrics. Make six sea gulls, following Steps 1–16 below and on page 74. *Note: Sea gulls are appliquéd in place after quilt has been assembled and machine-quilted.*

1 Seam pieces using ¼" seam allowance. Notch at center, press toward larger piece.

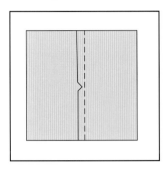

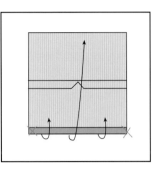

2 Press edge of larger piece under ¼". At folded edge, press in corners ¼". Trim corners of pressed-under edge. Fold in half at seam.

3 Press in half, then open.

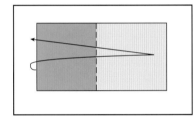

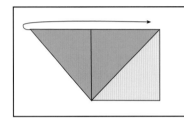

4 Bring upper-left corner to meet upper-right corner. Align centers. Press flat.

5 Crease on dotted line. Unfold.

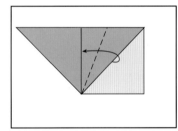

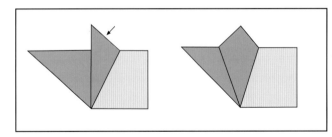

6 Lift corner, open and flatten.

7 Take upper point to bottom point. Use pins to help accentuate points.

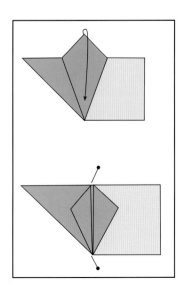

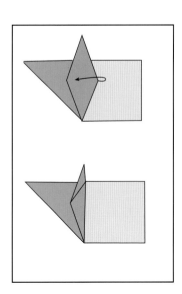

8 Fold lower point up, then fold right edge over onto left.

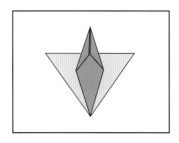 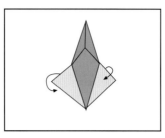 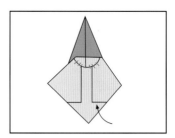

9 Repeat Steps 4–8 on page 73 with opposite side.

10 Fold upper corners under. Turn over.

11 Fold top diagonal corner down, tack in place. Cut away bottom points from top layer.

 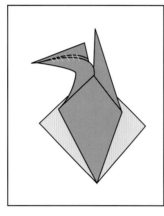 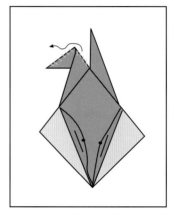

12 From back side, working with upper-left point, turn under raw edge. Hand-stitch.

13 Turn over, working from right side, hand-stitch upper-left point.

14 Fold upper-left point inward, forming bird's head. Hand-stitch. Fold front edge, hand-tack.

15 Stuff kite-shaped area lightly in front. Tack head. Stitch together, along with upper corner of kite-shaped area.

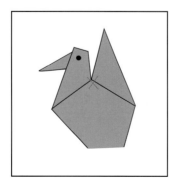

16 Tack head and tail together, along upper corner of kite-shaped area. Embroider eye.

BORDER & BACKING:

1 Cut three 3" x 40" strips from sage fabric. Stitch two pieces to quilt side, mitering bottom corner to match **Sea Gull Block** side. Stitch last strip to quilt-top edge.

2 Cut twenty 8" squares from four gold fabrics, and ecru fabric for backing. Alternately, stitch squares together, four per row, for total of five rows.

3 Layer backing, batting and quilt top. Pin-baste together. Free-motion machine-quilt. Do not quilt over seal, duckies, or quilted pockets.

4 Cut 1"-wide strips from blue fabric. Bind quilt with blue strips.

5 Appliqué top of seal to **Sunrise Block**. Wrap ribbons around chubby guys to cinch waists. Tie ribbon into bows. Arrange kites, kite strings, chubby guys, and toddlers, holding on to kite strings. Appliqué in place. Center and appliqué sea gulls to **Sea Gull Block**. Embroider eyes and whiskers on seal.

Come Play with Me Quilt Diagram

This chapter of unfinished blocks is packed full of ideas for fabric folding, pleating, and texturing. One of the groups of unfinished blocks focuses on creatures that swim in the deep blue sea or that fly among the clouds. The backdrops are an assembly of wonderful textures that are an inspirational resource. After noticing what kinds of creatures garnish the backdrops, you will be inspired to try your own hand with many different types of fabric-folded fish or fowl.

The second group of unfinished blocks focuses on simple geometric shapes inspired by common quilt blocks. By augmenting the basic seam of a quilt block with prairie points or by exposing an underlying surprise beneath turned-back folds, a fundamental quilt block can be seen through new eyes. Any simple quilt block can be approached in this manner. By taking a cue from ribbonwork, rudimentary box or knife pleats become unexpected textural elements among squares and rectangles.

The third group of unfinished blocks has been inspired by the timeless technique of crazy quilting—building random texture onto a foundation. The use of fancier, solid-toned fabrics causes these quilt blocks to be elegant and dramatic. They are further complemented with a variety of techniques inspired by a simple napkin fold or ribbonwork petals and leaves. Folded fabric scraps are arranged circularly, like the many-petaled layers of a garden rose, and a simple star shape becomes a dimensional star flower. May these unfinished blocks become finished masterpieces for you.

WITHOUT OARS YOU CANNOT CROSS RIVERS IN A BOAT.

CRANE BLOCK

FABRICS:

Blue (four different variations)
- Three variations of blue (½ yd each) for sky
- Blue (⅛ yd) for crane

Gold (two different variations)
- Bright gold (½ yd) for sky
- Gold (½ yd) for sky

Muslin (one variation)
- Muslin (½ yd) for foundation

Orange (two different variations)
- Coral (½ yd) for sky
- Orange (½ yd) for sky

Purple (two different variations)
- Purple (⅛ yd) for crane
- Purple (½ yd) for sky

CRANE BLOCK:

1 Cut 13" square from muslin for foundation. Using **Sky Diagram**, trace sky lines onto muslin.

2 Cut 3½" x 14" strips from eight sky-related fabrics.

3 Working in numerical sequence, place bright gold fabric onto first space. Trim excess fabric ¼" past sky line for first space.

4 Place gold fabric over bright gold, right sides together. Stitch straight edge of gold fabric to curved edge of bright gold fabric using ¼" seam allowance. Press gold fabric upward. Use steam and water-filled spray bottle to ease and direct gold fabric piece.

5 Trim excess gold fabric ¼" past sky line for second space.

6 Place coral fabric over gold fabric, right sides together. Stitch straight edge of coral fabric to curved edge of gold fabric, in same manner as in Step 4. Press coral fabric upward. Use steam and water-filled spray bottle to ease and direct coral fabric piece.

7 Trim excess coral fabric ¼" past sky line for third space.

8 Continue to stitch straight edges of remaining fabrics to curved edges of previous fabric to create sky backdrop as shown in photo on page 77. Trim block to desired size.

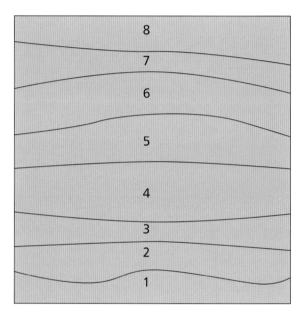

Sky Diagram

Tips:

This particular crane is the classic "flapping bird" that many of us learned to make as children. You can make the bird's wings flap in Step 7 of the Crane directions on the opposite page.

Imagine this bird made with larger pieces of fabric. It could be slightly stuffed, then hung from the ceiling in a child's room.

Crane:

Using one 8½" x 4½" piece from each blue fabric and purple fabric, make one crane, following Steps 1–9 below.

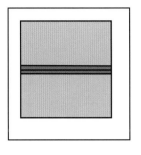 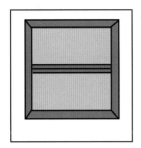

1 Seam together two rectangles. Press seam open.

2 Press under all edges ¼" to wrong side.

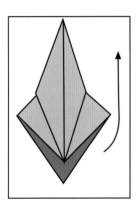 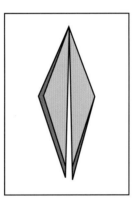 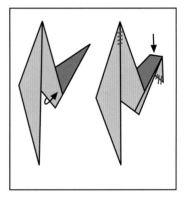

3 Fold into square. Refer to Snail, Steps 2–4 on page 44.

4 Lift bottom point up and press edges to center.

5 Turn over. Repeat Step 4.

6 Inside-reverse fold. Stitch. Fold point down.

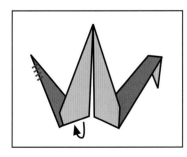 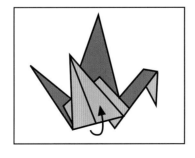

7 Inside-reverse fold. Stitch.

8 Fold up.

9 Appliqué crane to center of square.

CLOUDS BLOCK

FABRICS:

Blue (four different variations)

- Three variations of blue (¼ yd each) for sky, for clouds, for border
- Blue striped (⅛ yd) for border

Lavender (four different variations)

- Lavender striped (⅛ yd) for sky
- Two variations of lavender (⅛ yd each) for sky
- Lavender (⅛ yd) for borders

Purple (one variation)

- Purple (⅛ yd) for clouds

CLOUDS BLOCK:

1 Cut three 3½" x 12" strips from each sky fabric for knife pleats. Stitch strips together, using ¼" seam allow-ance. Press seam allowances open.

2 Using water-soluble pen, draw line onto fabrics 1½" below each seam. Crease fabric on each seam and on each drawn line. Press creases.

3 Working from bottom crease, fold fabric into ½"-deep pleat. Bring creased edge of pleat to ½" below next crease. Pin pleat in place along both edges.

Tips:

Circles are tricky to stitch, as they can tend to look more angular than cir-cular. But, by sewing with very small stitches, those pesky angles are greatly diminished.

Before turning the "clouds" right side out, open up the seam and press half of it flat (this is called edge-pressing). This step helps "expose" the seam when pressing from the right side.

4 Fold next creased edge (this will be a seamed crease) into ½"-deep pleat then bring creased edge to ½" below next crease. Pin pleat along both edges. Continue to knife-pleat creased fabric into ½"-deep pleats in this manner. Stitch pleats in place along side edges. Press pleats flat.

5 Cut five 2¾" circles, eleven 2¼" circles, and eight 1⅞" circles from cloud fabrics.

6 Cut each circle in half. Place two halves, right sides together. Using ⅛" seam allowance and very small stitch (1.5 metric), stitch curved edge. Turn half circle right side out. Press.

7 Slip circles within pleats up to inner folded edge. Lift pleat underneath bottommost cloud. Stitch on wrong side of pleat near folded underside edge, catching cloud in seam. Repeat with each additional cloud. *Note: Stitching will not be visible.*

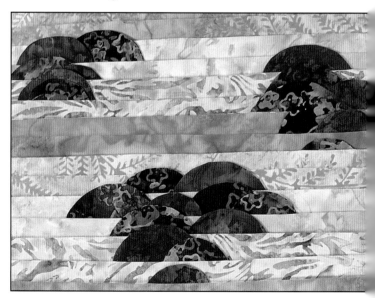

Circles in Pleats

8 Trim pleated piece to 10" x 12".

9 Cut 1½"–2½" strips for borders. Stitch strips to pleated piece as shown in **Clouds Block Diagram**. Trim excess fabric from border ½" past wavy line, creating curves. Stitch straight edge of one border piece to curved edge of previous border piece. Press. Trim new border, creating another curvy border. Continue to add curvy borders as desired.

10 Trim block to desired size.

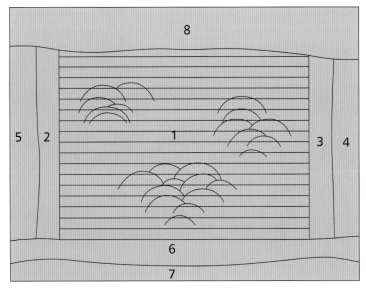

Clouds Block Diagram

Border

TROPICAL FISH BLOCK

TROPICAL FISH BLOCK:

1 Cut 12" x 14" piece from blue fabric for tucked space. Using water-soluble pen and ruler, draw diagonal lines onto fabric, as shown in **Background Diagram**. Press fabric on drawn line, then stitch ⅛" from creased edge, forming tuck. Press tuck upward. Continue to press on drawn lines and stitch ⅛" from creased edges. *Note: Finished piece will have an irregular shape. Use shape as is within block.*

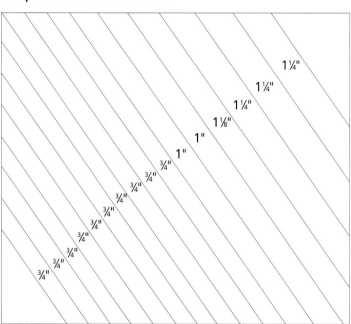

Background Diagram

Continued on page 86.

FABRICS:

Blue (two different variations)
- Blue (⅓ yd) for tucked piece of background
- Blue (⅛ yd) for bottom border of background

Coral (one variation)
- Coral (⅛ yd) for side and top borders of background

Green/tan (one variation)
- Green/tan (⅛ yd) for tropical fish

Lavender (one variation)
- Lavender (⅛ yd) for side borders, background

Orange/lime (one variation)
- Orange/lime (⅛ yd) for tropical fish

Continued from page 84.

2 Cut 1½"–3½" strips from border fabrics. Stitch strips to tucked piece as shown in **Strip Diagram**. To create curves, trim away excess fabric from border ¼" past wavy line. Stitch straight edge of one border piece to curved edge of previous border piece. Press, then trim new border in order to add another curvy border. *Note: Wider borders will have to be pleated slightly in order to lie flat.* Continue to add curvy borders as desired.

3 Trim block to desired size. Randomly turn tucks back and tack to look like waves and ripples.

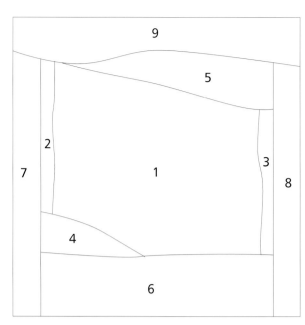

Strip Diagram

Tropical Fish:

Using two of **Pattern A**, orange/lime fabric, and green/tan fabric, make tropical fish, following Steps 1–12 on opposite page.

Pattern A
¼" seam allowance

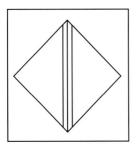 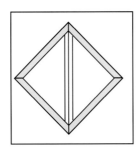 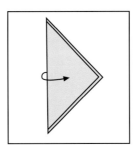 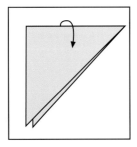

1 Seam two tri-angles together. Press open.

2 Press under all four edges ¼" to wrong side.

3 Press in half.

4 Press in half from a differ-ent direction.

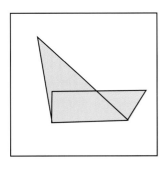 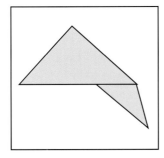 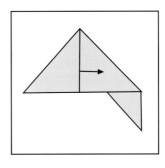 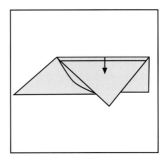

5 Press up on both sides.

6 Place in this position.

7 Fold center of bot-tom left tip to right. Turn over. Re-peat with other side.

8 Place in this po-sition. Fold upper triangle down.

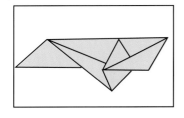 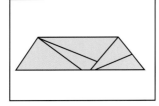 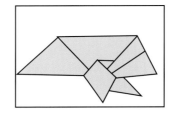 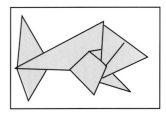

9 When upper tri-angle is folded down and flattened. Turn over and repeat on other side.

10 Tack corners under.

11 Bring down fins on both sides.

12 Separate tail pieces. Inside-reverse fold upper layer. Inside-reverse fold bottom layer up, then down. Appliqué tropical fish to block. Hand-tack some of tucks downward.

DOLPHIN BLOCK

FABRICS:

Blue (five different variations)
- Three variations of blue (⅛ yd each) for ocean
- Two variations of blue (⅛ yd each) for dolphin

Blue/green (one variation)
- Blue/green (⅛ yd) for ocean

Lavender (two different variations)
- Two variations of lavender (¼ yd each) for sky, for top border

Purple (one variation)
- Purple (⅛ yd) for dolphin

TROPICAL FISH BLOCK

1. For knife-pleated space, cut one 3½" x 12" strip from each ocean fabric, except cut 2½" x 12" strip from ocean blue fabric (uppermost pleated ocean fabric, also used for border). For sky, cut fabric 9" x 12". Stitch strips together, using ¼" seam allowance. Stitch sky fabric to top edge of uppermost ocean fabric. Press seam allowances open.

2. Using water-soluble pen, draw a line onto ocean fabrics 1½" from each seam. Press fabric over on each seam and on each drawn line.

3. Working from bottom crease, fold fabric into ½"-deep pleat, bringing folded edge of pleat to ½" below next crease. Pin pleat in place along both edges.

4. Fold next creased edge (this will be a seamed crease) into ½"-deep pleat, then bring folded edge up to ½" below the next crease. Pin pleat along both edges. Continue to knife-pleat creased fabric into ½"-deep pleats in this manner. Stitch pleats in place along side edges, then press pleats flat.

5. Cut eight 2½" squares from ocean fabrics. Press squares into prairie point as shown in **Prairie Point Diagram**.

Prairie Point Diagram

6. Refer to photo on opposite page for placement, slip prairie points within pleats up to inner folded edge. Lift pleat underneath bottommost triangle and stitch triangle to pleat near folded underside edge. Repeat with each additional triangle. *Note: Stitching will not be visible.*

7. Using water soluble pen, draw line onto sky 1" from sky/ocean seam. Draw five more lines onto sky 1¼" apart. Press fabric on drawn line then stitch ¼" from creased edge, forming tuck. Press tuck upward. Continue to press on drawn lines and stitch ¼" from creased edges.

8. Trim block to 12" x 10".

9. Cut 1½"–3½" strips for borders. Stitch strips to pleated and tucked piece as shown in **Strip Diagram** on page 90. To create curves, trim excess fabric from border ¼" past wavy line. Stitch straight edge of one border piece to curved edge of previous border piece. Press, then trim

Continued on page 90.

Continued from page 88.

new border in order to add another curvy border. *Note: Wider borders may have to be pleated slightly in order to lie flat.* Continue to add curvy borders as desired.

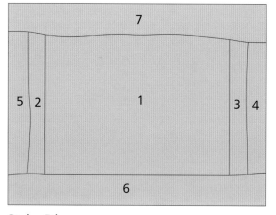

Strip Diagram

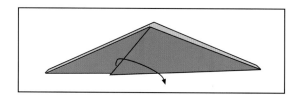

10 Trim block to desired size.

Dolphin:

1 Using two of **Pattern A**, **Pattern B**, two blue fabrics, and one purple fabric, stitch As and B piece together as shown in **Dolphin Square Diagram**.

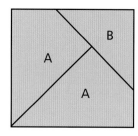

Dolphin Square Diagram

2 Using Dolphin Square, make dolphin by completing Seal Steps 1–7 on pages 62–63, then follow Steps 3–14 below and on opposite page.

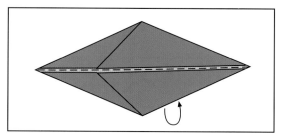

3 Fold in half.

4 Fold down for fin.

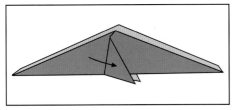

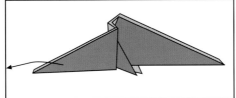

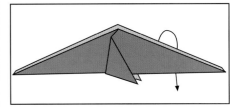

5 Repeat for other fin. Shape each side differently so they show.

6 Pleat back, press and unfold.

7 Open out.

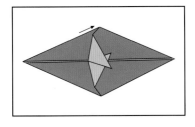

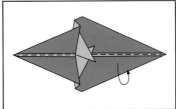

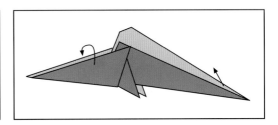

8 Refold on pleat made in Step 4 on opposite page.

9 Fold in half again.

10 Fold upper flap inward. Fold left side to back diagonally. Make inside-reverse fold with right side.

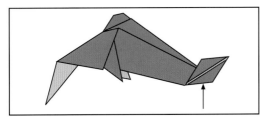

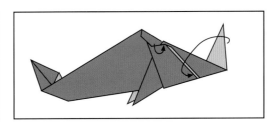

11 Flatten right side, forming tail. Turn over.

12 Fold tip into pocket on back.

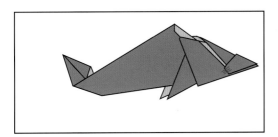

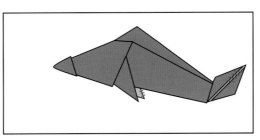

13 Stitch at pocket.

14 Stitch tail and ends of fins.

PEELED-ORANGE BLOCK

FABRICS:

<u>Coral (one variation)</u>
- Coral (¼ yd) for 6" squares

<u>Ecru/green (one variation)</u>
- Ecru/green (¼ yd) for Pattern C

<u>Green (one variation)</u>
- Green (¼ yd) for Pattern C

<u>Orange (one variation)</u>
- Orange (¼ yd) for Pattern B

<u>Yellow (one variation)</u>
- Yellow (⅛ yd) for border

NOTIONS:

Cover button: ⅝" dia.

Tip:

The Peeled-orange Block presented here is an enhanced variation of the classic Orange Peel Block introduced in 1898, also known as Melon Patch. The center wedge in each 4-patch was the obvious location to integrate fabric folds. Rather than having only two layers to stitch together, the folded fabric layers totaled seven. Tracing the wedge shape onto the layered section, then sewing on the traced line, made piecing the block a simple task.

PEELED-ORANGE BLOCK:

Note: Enlarge all patterns and templates 200%.

1 Cut four of **Pattern C** from green fabric. Cut four of **Pattern C** from ecru/green fabric for each of two of 4-patch designs.

2 Cut four 6" squares from coral fabric. Cut four of **Pattern B** from orange fabric and ecru/green fabric.

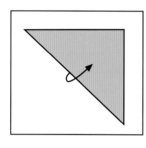

3 Press one 6" square in half diagonally.

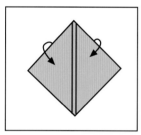

4 Press ends in for square fold.

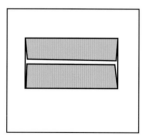

5 Press two orange C pieces in half. Place on top of right side of green C with folded edges, meeting along center.

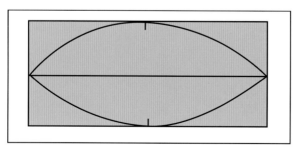

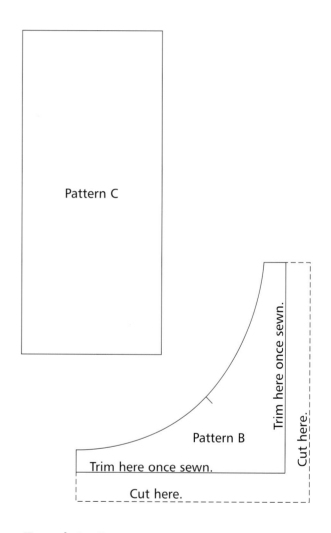

Pattern C

Trim here once sewn.

Cut here.

Pattern B

Trim here once sewn.

Cut here.

6 Trace **Template A** on opposite page onto pieces from Step 4. Slip folded square within wedge layers. Stitch inside traced lines ⅛" from edges.

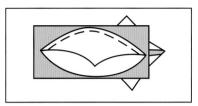

7 Stitch with right sides together, using curved edges of ecru/green Bs to each side of wedge, matching cut edges of B with traced line of A. Stitch through all layers.

8 Repeat Steps 3–7 on page 94 and above to make a second patch with same coloration. Make two more patches with contrasting coloration.

9 Trim bulk within layers by grading. Use **Template D** to square up each patch by placing curved edge along sewn wedge edge.

10 Stitch patches together and press seams open as shown in **Peeled-orange Block Diagram**.

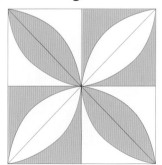

Peeled-orange Block Diagram

11 Stitch ⅝" cover button in center.

12 Press inside of wedge back ¼" to reveal inside. Tack at center of turned back edge of wedge.

13 Cut four 2½" squares from green fabric for border corners. Cut four 2½" x 8½" strips from yellow fabric for border sides.

14 Stitch square to each end of two strips. Stitch strips without ends to block. Stitch strips with ends to block.

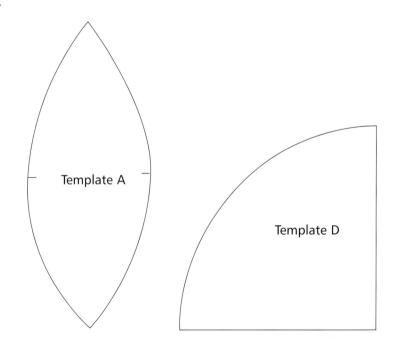

Border

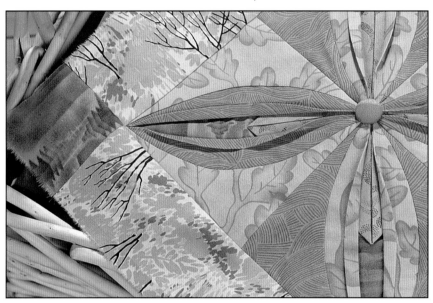

Template A

Template D

KEY WEST BEAUTY BLOCK

FABRICS:

Blue (one variation)
- Blue (⅛ yd) for prairie points, border

Brown (one variation)
- Brown (⅛ yd) for 2¾" squares

Gold (two different variations)
- Gold (⅛ yd) for Pattern A1, Pattern A2, Pattern A3
- Gold (⅛ yd) for Pattern B

Green (one variation)
- Green (⅛ yd) for 2¾" squares, border

Teal (one variation)
- Teal (⅛ yd) for Pattern D

KEY WEST BEAUTY BLOCK:

1 Cut four each of **Pattern A1**, **Pattern A2**, and **Pattern A3** from pale gold fabric. Cut four 2" squares, four 2¼" squares, and four 2½" squares from blue fabric.

2 Cut four of **Pattern B** from bright gold fabric.

3 Cut four 2¾" squares from green fabric, and eight from brown fabric.

4 Cut four of **Pattern D** on opposite page from teal fabric.

5 Fold each pale blue square as a prairie point as shown in **Prairie Point Diagram**.

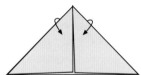

Prairie Point Diagram

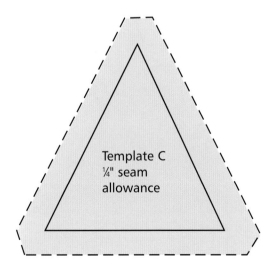

Template C
¼" seam allowance

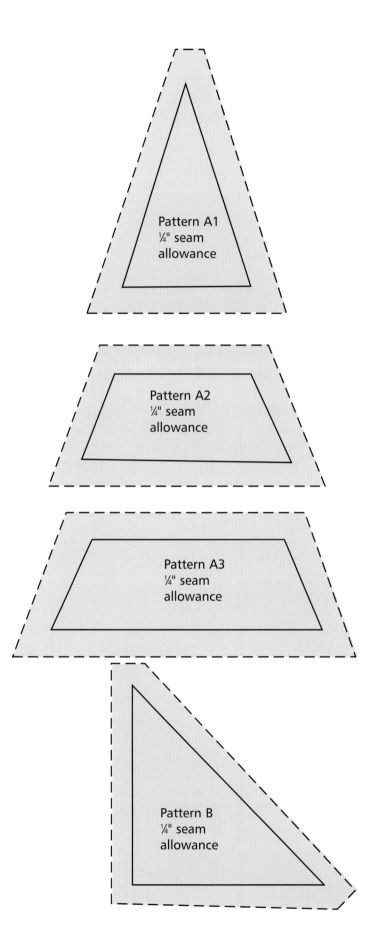

Pattern A1
¼" seam allowance

Pattern A2
¼" seam allowance

Pattern A3
¼" seam allowance

Pattern B
¼" seam allowance

6 Stitch 2½" prairie point to bottom edge of A3. Stitch 2¼" prairie point between A3 and A2. Stitch 2" prairie point between A2 and A1. Stitch B to each assembled A as shown in **Assembled A Diagram**.

7 Press two brown squares pieces in half. Place on green square with folded edges toward each other in center.

8 Trace **Template C** on page 100 onto folded pieces. Stitch inside traced lines ⅛" from edges. Trim C to traced lines.

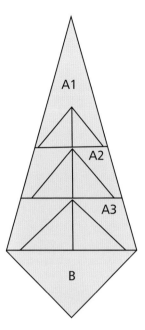

Assembled A Diagram

9 Stitch C to each side of D. Stitch assembled D to **Assembled A** as shown in **Key West Block Diagram**.

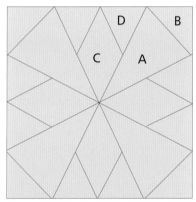

Key West Block Diagram

10 Cut four 2½" squares from blue fabric for corners. Cut 2½" x 8½" strips from green fabric for sides.

11 Stitch squares to each end of two strips. Stitch strips without ends to block. Stitch strips with ends to block.

Assembled A

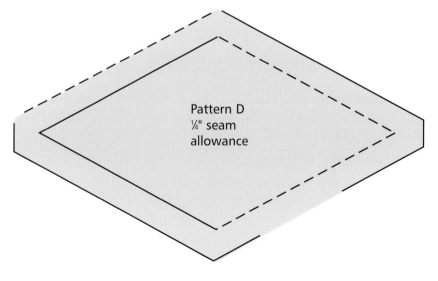

Pattern D
¼" seam allowance

BOX-PLEAT BLOCK

FABRICS:

<u>Blue (one variation)</u>
- Blue (⅛ yd) for border

<u>Coral (one variation)</u>
- Coral (⅛ yd) for box pleats

<u>Green (one variation)</u>
- Green (⅛ yd) for base squares

<u>Orange (one variation)</u>
- Orange (⅛ yd) for box pleats

<u>Tan/green (one variation)</u>
- Tan/green (⅛ yd) for borders

<u>Yellow (one variation)</u>
- Yellow (⅛ yd) for base squares underneath box pleats

Fabric Variations

BOX-PLEAT BLOCK:

1 Cut eight 2½" squares from green fabric for base squares and eight 2½" squares from yellow fabric for base squares underneath box pleats.

2 Cut seven 2" x 6⅜" pieces from orange fabric, seven 3" x 6⅜" pieces from coral fabric for seven box-pleated pieces.

3 Cut 2" x 6⅜" piece from blue fabric and 3" x 6⅜" piece from yellow fabric for one box-pleated piece.

4 Working with orange and coral fabrics, stitch pieces, right sides together, stitching long edges and taking a ¼" seam allowance. Press seam allowances open and turn tube right side out. Press well. Repeat seven times for eight tubes (seven orange/coral and one blue/yellow).

5 Using ruler and water-soluble pen, draw pleating lines on bordered side of each tube, beginning and ending ⅜" from each cut end as shown in **Pleating Diagram**.

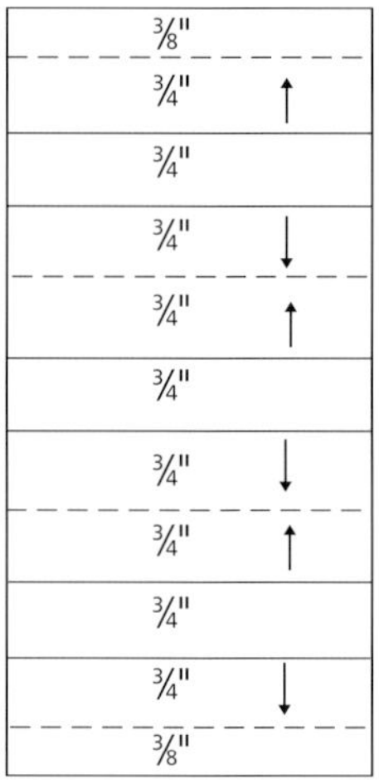

⅜"		
¾"		↑
¾"		
¾"		↓
¾"		↑
¾"		
¾"		↓
¾"		↑
¾"		
¾"		↓
⅜"		

Pleating Diagram

6 Stitch one row of 16-patch together, alternating yellow and green squares. Repeat, making four rows but not stitching rows together.

7 Pin one edge of two tubes to bottom edge of yellow squares for first row. Pin one edge of two tubes to top edge of yellow squares for second row.

8 Stitch first and second rows, with right sides together, facing taking a ¼" seam allowance. Repeat with third and fourth rows.

9 Working with tubes on second row, pin bottom edge of tubes to bottom edge of yellow squares. Working with tubes on third row, pin top edge of tubes to top edge of yellow squares. Stitch second and third rows together. Press seam allowances downward.

10 Cut four 2½" squares from blue fabric for corners. Cut four 2½" x 8½" strips from blue fabric for sides.

11 Stitch squares to each end of two strips. Stitch strips without ends to block. Stitch strips with ends to block. Catch bottom edge of tubes on first row in with border when stitching. Catch bottom edge of tubes on fourth row in with border when stitching. Take care to not catch tube sides in with border.

12 Box-pleat tubes, bringing solid lines to dotted lines. Stitch down center to secure box pleats.

Completed Box Pleats

Box Pleats

13 Spray marks with water to erase.

Tip:

Making the tube so that it has contrasting fabric edges accomplishes two things, other than creating finished edges: It eliminates the bulk that would have been created by a seam at the edges and it draws attention to itself, causing the box pleats to be more visible.

KNIFE-PLEAT BLOCK

FABRICS:

Blue (two different variations)
- Blue (⅛ yd) for Pattern B
- Blue (⅛ yd) for border

Brown (one variation)
- Brown (¼ yd) for tube edge

Gold (one variation)
- Gold (¼ yd) for tube edge

Green (one variation)
- Green (⅛ yd) for tube

Multiprint (one variation)
- Multiprint (⅛ yd) for Pattern A

Teal (one variation)
- Teal (⅛ yd) for tube

Yellow (one variation)
- Yellow (⅛ yd) for Pattern B

Fabric Variations

KNIFE-PLEAT BLOCK:

1 Cut four of **Pattern A** on opposite page from multiprint fabric for base underneath knife-pleated pieces. Cut four of **Pattern B** on opposite page from yellow fabric and cut four of **Pattern B** from blue fabric for base squares.

2 Cut two 2" x 12¾" strips from green fabric and two 2" x 12¾" strips from teal fabric for knife-pleated pieces. Cut two 3" x 12¾" strips from pale gold and two 3" x 12¾" strips from brown fabric for knife-pleated pieces.

3 Stitch one brown strip to one teal strip with right sides together, taking a ¼" seam allowance and stitching long edges for tube. Repeat for one gold strip and one green strip. Press seam allowances open and turn tubes right side out. Press well. Repeat for remaining strips for four tubes.

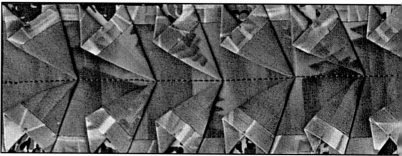

Tubes

4 Using ruler and water-soluble pen, draw pleating lines on bordered side of each tube, beginning and ending ⅜" from each cut end as shown in **Pleating Diagram**.

5 Stitch four sets of two contrasting Bs together. Stitch A to assembled Bs, with one end of tube sandwiched between A and B square as shown in **Knife-pleat Block Diagram**. Repeat to make four 2½" x 8½" strips. Stitch four strips together for block, alternating positions of As and Bs. Take care to not catch sides of tube in seams. Press seams open.

Pleating Diagram

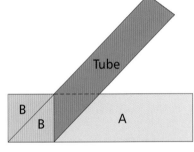

Knife-pleat Block Diagram

6 Cut two 2½" x 8½" strips from blue fabric. Cut two 2½" x 12¼" strips from blue fabric.

7 Stitch 8½" strips to top and bottom of block. Catch loose end of tubes in with border when stitching. Stitch 12¼" strips to sides. Take note to not catch sides of tubes in with border.

8 Knife-pleat tubes, bringing solid lines to dotted lines. Stitch down center to secure knife pleats.

9 Press folded edge of each knife pleat back and flatten as shown in **Folding Diagram**. Hand-tack folds in place.

10 Spray marks with water to erase.

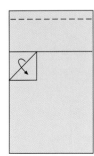

Folding Diagram

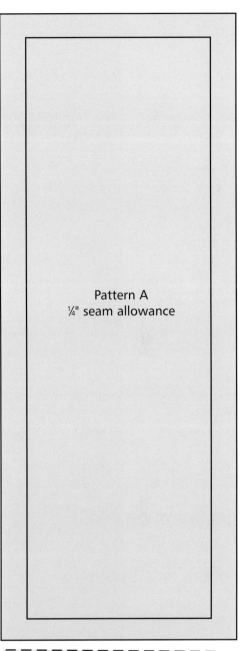

Pattern A
¼" seam allowance

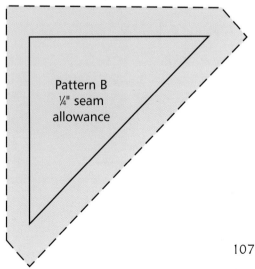

Pattern B
¼" seam allowance

NAPKIN-FOLD BLOCK

Green striped (one variation)
- Green striped (¼ yd) for background foundation

Red/gold striped metallic (one variation)
- Red/gold striped metallic (¼ yd) for napkin fold

Sheer metallic (one variation)
- Sheer metallic (¼ yd) for block front

Scraps (nine different variations)
- Nine variations of scraps for crazy strips

Muslin (one variation)
- Muslin (⅛ yd) for background

NAPKIN-FOLD BLOCK:

Note: Enlarge all patterns 200%.

1 Cut four of **Pattern E** from green striped fabric. Stitch Es together. Cut sheer metallic fabric large enough to cover over sewn Es. Place sheer fabric over pieced block.

2 Using muslin as a foundation, stitch crazy strips around block in numerical sequence as shown in **Crazy Strip Diagram**. Trim to size.

Tip:

The striped fabric used for Pattern E was a little strong, as it competed with the stripe used for the napkin fold. By laying the sheer metallic fabric over the "backdrop," the stripe was toned down and a new, interesting texture was created.

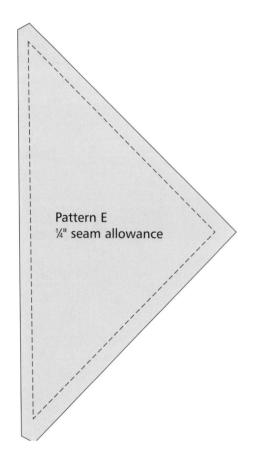

Pattern E
¼" seam allowance

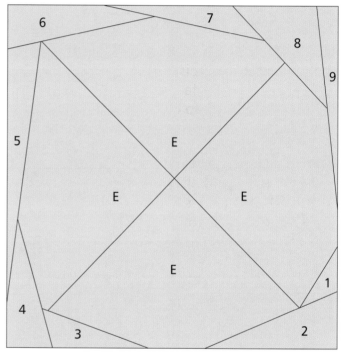

Crazy Strip Diagram

Tip:

Do you have a favorite napkin-folding book or resource? Many classic napkin-folding techniques would be suitable for enhancing a "crazy" backdrop. The raw edges of fabric could be finished in the same manner as for this napkin fold. An alternative would be to narrowly hem the raw edges of a fabric square before folding it into shape.

Napkin Fold:

Using 7½" x 14½" piece from red/gold metallic fabric, make one napkin fold, following Steps 1–5 below.

1 Fold fabric in half. Stitch three sides, leaving opening to turn. Trim corners. Edge-press. Turn right side out. Press.

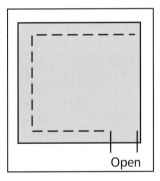

2 Fold points to center. Stitch over point without stitching through bottom layer.

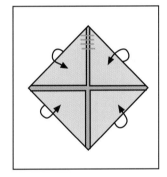

3 Fold points to center again. Turn over.

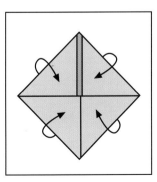

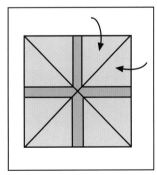

4 Fold points to center. Tack center tips together.

5 Pull out tips from bottom.

PLEATED PETALS BLOCK

FABRICS:

Green sheer metallic (one variation)
- Green sheer metallic (⅛ yd) for stem

Orange metallic (one variation)
- Orange metallic (3" circle) for yo-yo

Muslin (one variation)
- Muslin (¼ yd) for foundation fabric

Remnants (six different variations)
- Six variations of remnants (⅛ yd each) for piecing

White organza (one variation)
- White organza (⅛ yd) for pleated petals, rosebuds

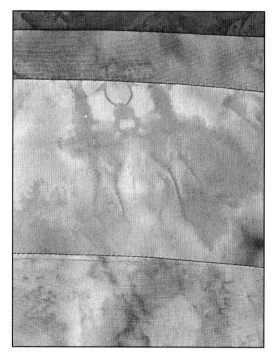

Fabric Variations

PLEATED PETALS BLOCK:

1 Cut 9" square from muslin for foundation fabric. Stitch assorted remnants onto foundation, following numerical sequence in **Piecing Diagram**.

2 Cut four ¾" x 12" bias strips from sheer metallic fabric. Twist bias tightly and knot every 3". Use to appliqué center leaf loops onto pieced fabric as shown in **Stem Bias Diagram**.

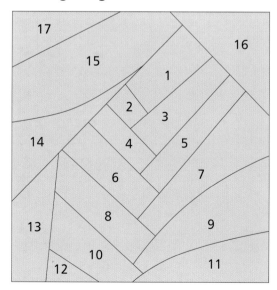

Piecing Diagram

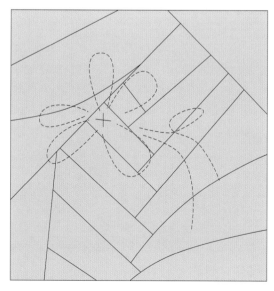

Stem Bias Diagram

Rosebuds:

Using remaining two strips, make two rosebuds, following Steps 1–2 below.

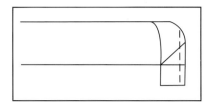

1 Turn under end two times. Fold down, then fold over ⅛", leaving a tail. Begin to roll.

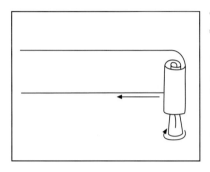

2 Continue to roll. When almost to end, roll end downward. Secure by stitching at bottom. Wrap end of one twisted bias strip around raw edges of rosebud. Hand-stitch in place.

Rosebuds & Pleated Petals

Pleated Petals:

Cut seven 3" x 7" strips from white organza. Fold strips in half and stitch long edges, taking a ¼" seam allowance. Turn strips right side out and press, placing seamline ¼" from one folded edge. Make five pleated petals, following Steps 1–3 below and at right.

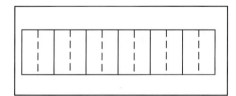

1 Pleat mountain-and-valley folds ¼" apart. Slightly offsetting pleat at bottom edge.

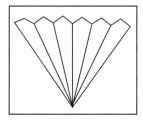

2 Using needle and thread, secure folds at bottom. Stitch pleated petals in flower shape to block.

3 Hand-stitch rosebud with stem onto pieced fabric. Overlap pleated petals and hand-stitch to pieced fabric over leaves.

4 Cut 2¾" circle from orange metallic fabric.

5 Using needle and thread, running-stitch around edge of circle about ⅛" from edge. When completely around circle, pull thread to gather edges in for yo-yo. Tie off and cut thread.

6 Stitch yo-yo over center of flower, covering all raw edges.

STAR FLOWER BLOCK

FABRICS:

Green sheer metallic (two different variations)

- Two variations of green sheer metallic (⅛ yd each) for leaves, stems

Mauve velvet (one variation)

- Mauve velvet (⅛ yd) for yo-yo

Muslin (one variation)

- Muslin (¼ yd) for foundation

Orange metallic (one variation)

- Orange (¼ yd) for block sides

Pink (two different variations)

- Two variations of pink (⅛ yd each) for star flower

Scraps (seven different variations)

- Seven variations of scraps for piecing

NOTIONS:

Quilt batting

STAR FLOWER BLOCK:

1 Cut 9" x 13" piece from muslin for foundation fabric. Stitch assorted scraps onto foundation, following numerical sequence as shown in **Piecing Diagram**.

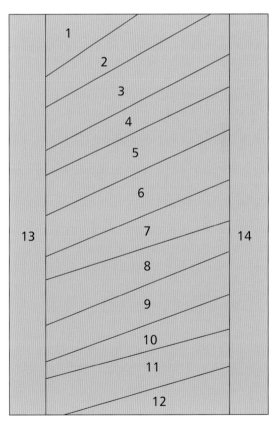

Piecing Diagram

Leaf:

Using 2¾" circles cut from green sheer metallic fabric, make six leaves, following Steps 1–3 below.

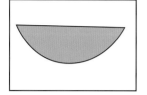 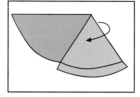

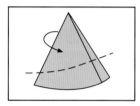

1 Fold circle in half.

2 Fold folded edge down.

3 Fold opposite edge down. Gather along edges. Repeat five times for six leaves.

Stem:

1 Cut four ¾" x 12" bias strips from green sheer metallic fabric for stem. Twist bias tightly and knot every 3".

2 Wrap end of twisted bias strip around raw edges of one leaf. Hand-stitch bias in place, finishing raw edges. Hand-stitch leaf and stem onto pieced fabric.

3 Position remaining two leaves on fabric near desired flower position. Repeat Step 2 with a second bias strip, adding two more leaves to this bias strip. Entwine second bias strip around first and hand-stitch stem with leaves in place on pieced fabrics.

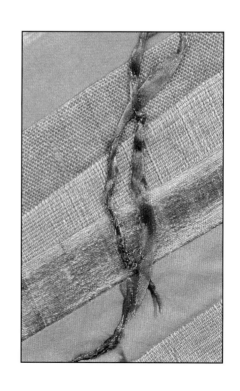

Star Flower:

Note: Enlarge pattern 200%.

Using **Pattern A** and pink fabrics, make two star flowers, following Steps 1–3 below.

Star Flower with Yo-yo

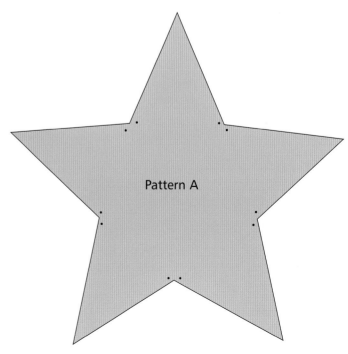

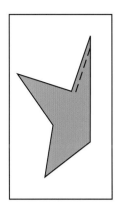 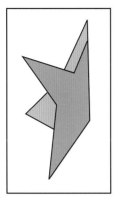 

1 Fold one point in half, matching dots. Stitch from dot to tip.

2 Fold next point in half. Stitch dot to tip. Repeat with each point.

3 Turn right side out. Stuff lightly.

Yo-yo:

1 Cut 3½" circle from mauve velvet fabric.

2 Using needle and thread, running-stitch around edge of circle ⅛" from edge. When completely around circle, pull thread to gather edges in for yo-yo. Tie off and cut thread.

3 Stuff yo-yo, then secure with stitches.

4 Overlap two **Star Flowers**, off-setting petals. Stitch stuffed yo-yo to center of flowers, stitching some of top petal layers to center of yo-yo.

5 Stitch flower in place on pieced fabric. Stitch remaining bias strip to block sides.

Pattern A

119

ROSE BLOCK

FABRICS:

Green (three different variations)
- Two variations of green (scraps) for leaves
- Green (⅛ yd) for block

Lavender/gray (seven different variations)
- Seven variations of lavender/gray (scraps) for rose

Muslin (one variation)
- Muslin (¼ yd) for foundation

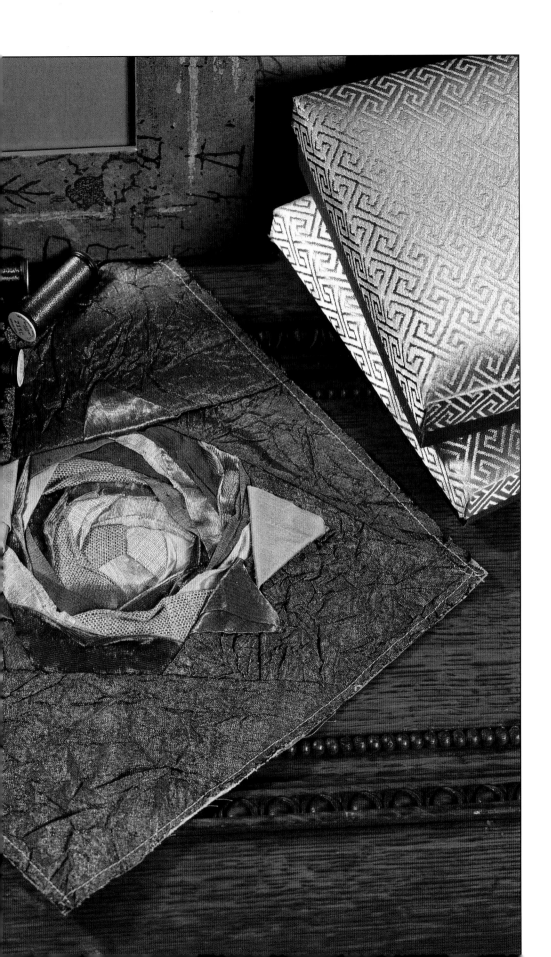

Piecing Diagram

ROSE BLOCK:

1 Cut 9" square from muslin for found-ation fabric.

2 Refer to **Piecing Diagram** for Steps 2–5. Cut 2" x 3" pieces from lavender/gray fabrics for center, overlapping #1 layers. Press fabric pieces in half, aligning 3" sides. Overlap onto found-ation in #1 positions. Pin pieces in place. Trace 2½" circle around pieces. Stitch on traced line. Trim excess fabric close to stitching.

3 Cut 3" squares from lavender/gray fabrics for #2 layers. Press in half. Overlap onto foundation in #2 positions. Trace 3" circle around #2 pieces. Stitch on traced line. Trim excess fabric close to stitching.

4 Cut 3" x 4" pieces from lavender/gray fabrics for #3 and #4 layers. Press in half, aligning 3" sides. Overlap onto foundation in #3 and #4 positions. Trace 4" circle around #3 and #4 pieces. Stitch and trim as before.

122

5 Cut 3" x 4" pieces from lavender/gray fabrics for #5 layers. Press in half, aligning 3" sides. Overlap in #5 positions.

Leaf:

Using 3" x 5" pieces and green fabrics, make five leaves, following Steps 1–2 below.

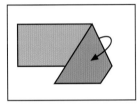 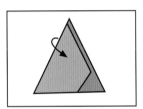

1 Fold piece in half, aligning 3" sides. Fold right side over.

2 Fold left side over and press.

3 Foundation-piece background fabric around rose, inserting a leaf where designated while stitching background pieces in place. Fold tip of leaf down and tack in place.

Tips:

The trick to making the Rose Block is making certain to hide the raw edges from the previous row when adding the next row. The placement of the pieces could be anywhere and the sizes of the pieces are arbitrary as well.

This would be a terrific block worked "oversized," you know—bigger than life.

This snail was created using the instructions on pages 44–46 and coordinating fabrics. Spray starch is the key trick to making the folded snail look so wonderful. Once all the folding and tacking has been finished and the snail's shell puffed, carefully arrange the shell's pleats and tack each pleat individually in place. Keep in mind that a 22" square of fabric will create an 11"-long snail.

125

ABOUT THE AUTHOR

Mary Jo Hiney works as a free-lance author, designer, and project contributor in the fabric and craft industry, gladly sharing skill-filled secrets gathered over a lifetime of experience. She is an expert seamstress and credits her solid sewing foundation to her mom, who had learned to sew in junior high from a very strict teacher. Mary Jo credits her love for quilting to her sister, Rose. It was Rose, whose love for projects that require detail and precision, laid the foundation for Mary Jo's knowledge of piecing and quilting some 25 years ago. It was Rose who first took Mary Jo to a fabric store that specialized in quilting fabrics, and it was Rose who helped Mary Jo make her first quilt. What better gift could a sister give?

Dedication:

For Rose, always my inspirational trailblazer.

Mary Jo would like to offer her sincere appreciation for the valuable support given in this ever-changing industry of new ideas, concepts, designs, and products. Several fabrics shown in this publication were created with outstanding and innovative products developed by Hoffman California Fabrics, Hoffman International Fabrics, 25792 Obrero Drive, Mission Viejo, CA 92691-3140, web site: www.hoffmanfabrics.com; and P & B Textiles, 1580 Gilbreth Road, Burlingame, CA 94010 web site: www.pbtex.com

METRIC CONVERSION CHARTS

mm-millimetres cm-centimetres
inches to millimetres and centimetres

inches	mm	cm	inches	cm	inches	cm
⅛	3	0.3	9	22.9	30	76.2
¼	6	0.6	10	25.4	31	78.7
⅜	10	1.0	11	27.9	32	81.3
½	13	1.3	12	30.5	33	83.8
⅝	16	1.6	13	33.0	34	86.4
¾	19	1.9	14	35.6	35	88.9
⅞	22	2.2	15	38.1	36	91.4
1	25	2.5	16	40.6	37	94.0
1¼	32	3.2	17	43.2	38	96.5
1½	38	3.8	18	45.7	39	99.1
1¾	44	4.4	19	48.3	40	101.6
2	51	5.1	20	50.8	41	104.1
2½	64	6.4	21	53.3	42	106.7
3	76	7.6	22	55.9	43	109.2
3½	89	8.9	23	58.4	44	111.8
4	102	10.2	24	61.0	45	114.3
4½	114	11.4	25	63.5	46	116.8
5	127	12.7	26	66.0	47	119.4
6	152	15.2	27	68.6	48	121.9
7	178	17.8	28	71.1	49	124.5
8	203	20.3	29	73.7	50	127.0

yards to metres

yards	metres	yards	metres	yards	metres	yards	metres	yards	metres
⅛	0.11	2⅛	1.94	4⅛	3.77	6⅛	5.60	8⅛	7.43
¼	0.23	2¼	2.06	4¼	3.89	6¼	5.72	8¼	7.54
⅜	0.34	2⅜	2.17	4⅜	4.00	6⅜	5.83	8⅜	7.66
½	0.46	2½	2.29	4½	4.11	6½	5.94	8½	7.77
⅝	0.57	2⅝	2.40	4⅝	4.23	6⅝	6.06	8⅝	7.89
¾	0.69	2¾	2.51	4¾	4.34	6¾	6.17	8¾	8.00
⅞	0.80	2⅞	2.63	4⅞	4.46	6⅞	6.29	8⅞	8.12
1	0.91	3	2.74	5	4.57	7	6.40	9	8.23
1⅛	1.03	3⅛	2.86	5⅛	4.69	7⅛	6.52	9⅛	8.34
1¼	1.14	3¼	2.97	5¼	4.80	7¼	6.63	9¼	8.46
1⅜	1.26	3⅜	3.09	5⅜	4.91	7⅜	6.74	9⅜	8.57
1½	1.37	3½	3.20	5½	5.03	7½	6.86	9½	8.69
1⅝	1.49	3⅝	3.31	5⅝	5.14	7⅝	6.97	9⅝	8.80
1¾	1.60	3¾	3.43	5¾	5.26	7¾	7.09	9¾	8.92

INDEX